BASIC
Transportation

ADVENTURES OF BAD LUCK
OWNING JUNK CARS

P.J. LAMB

Published by Simon Publishing LLC ®

Simon Publishing LLC is a registered trademark.
https://www.simonpublishingllc.com/

ISBN: 979-8-9894345-9-6

Library of Congress Control Number: 2025905217

Cover Design by Melissa Waters
www.anauthenticadventure.com

Printed by Ingram Spark
First Ed

2 0 2 5 0 4 1 0

DEDICATION

This book is dedicated to Pete Vander Voort (1946-2023).

CONTENTS

ACKNOWLEDGEMENTS

I would like to thank the people who supported, encouraged, un-knowingly contributed, edited or gave advice to this work. This includes, in alphabetical order:

Dan Barbush

Tara Bess

Mary Bolton

Allen Camp

Mark Cooke (co-editor)

Bill Ferris

Dennis Lamb

Pam Lamb

Sandy Lee

Jack O'Brien

Mark McKenna

Randy Proctor

Pete Vander Voort

Melissa Waters (co-editor)

BASIC
Transportation

ADVENTURES OF BAD LUCK
OWNING JUNK CARS

P.J. LAMB

SIMON PUBLISHING

CHAPTER 1

1968-1971: The Lambmobile

I was lying in bed on a hot August night in 1968 thinking in a stream of consciousness, *"What a freakin' toad I am. I have GOT to get a car! I'm in my twenties and all the other guys I know have wheels. Hell, I haven't even had a bike for 5 years. I got a driver's permit when I was 16, and didn't even get a license until a couple of years later. Just about every cent I made from part-time and summer jobs has gone toward college expenses. It makes me wonder if it's all been worth the tradeoff: taking buses, bumming rides from friends, driving Mom's car either when I'm home for the summer, or during other vacation breaks from school. Better than getting drafted and risking getting shot up in Vietnam, I guess. But no wonder I have a social life that's zero."* I slowly drifted off to sleep, dreaming about roaring around town in a GTO or Mustang.

The time was right. The next day after dinner I read an ad in the local paper about an upcoming auction for older NY State cars in Albany – about 50 vehicles of all shapes and sizes for sale at the Department of Transportation at noon on the 26th. Early the next evening, I took a walk up the street to my friend Pender's house. He was just coming out the back door when I got near there, and I yelled, "Hey, Pender – where you been all summer?"

"Working – same as you. But I work days, and you work 3-11. Hey, let's take a walk to Fox's. I have to get a 6-pack of beer. I don't want to go to Margie's (a bar a few blocks away)"

"Sounds good. I'll get some Schlitz myself. I never did like Margie's."

As we walked, we made small talk about our upcoming semesters in school, our jobs, and whether we'd seen any neighborhood kids we grew up with lately. I told him about the state car auction and how I was hoping to buy a car.

I said, "I've saved up $500 that I can afford to spend on a second-hand car."

He responded, "I'm off Tuesday and Wednesday. I'm looking for another car myself. Let's go over there together."

"Great!" I replied. "Can you drive us there? They'll have a list of all the cars, make, year, color, what department used them, and the mileage. And they give you an hour before the auction starts to check 'em out, but the downside is you can't drive 'em."

"Cool! Maybe we'll get lucky. I can drive us over. If I don't see any I like, my college roommate's brother will sell me one cheap in a few weeks when I get to Maryland. I'm tired of driving my father's old '60 Pontiac."

The big day came, and the weather was beautiful - 80 degrees and sunny. "Great day for buying a used car without some sleazy salesman pressuring you," I thought. Pender drove us over to the grassy lot where the cars were lined up. Almost every vehicle was black. They all had automatic transmissions, which helped because I didn't know a damn thing about a standard shift other than somehow you had to use a clutch to shift gears. In fact, the only things I knew about cars besides driving, braking, shifting gears and parking were how to pump gas, open the hood, check the oil, and change a tire.

There were about 75 people of various ages, races and sizes roaming around when we got there, checking out the cars and scribbling notes about the cars on which they were about to bid from the list and lot numbers. The lists, which were printed on two-sided sheets of paper, were given to everyone who wanted to bid on the vehicles. A small, open-ended old eight-row grandstand stood about 30 yards away from the cars. At the auctioneer's table, a chunky guy dressed in western style with a 10-gallon hat was arguing in a fairly loud voice with an elderly bespectacled man sporting a suit and checkered shirt.

As Pender and I meandered about the cars, marking our sheets in pen to note the cars we would bid on, Tim, the auctioneer (Mr. 10-gallon hat) came up to us with a big wide smile and said, "Hey, boys – how'd you like to make 50 bucks each? All you have to do is drive the cars up in front of the grandstand, put 'em in Park with the engine running, get out and stand next to 'em. When the bidding is over, I'll say, *'Roll the car, get it out of here.'* Then you'll drive it back to the lot and my man in the blue sweatshirt over there will give you the keys to the next one up. You'll do it two cars at a time, so the next car is waiting around 50 feet or so right in back of the first one we're auctioning."

Pender eagerly exclaimed, "Sounds great, sir!"

I chimed in, "Yeah, we'll do it!"

"We'll get you out of here no later than 3 o'clock. If you buy a car, then stick around. Like we said in the ad in the paper, you can either pay for it all today or put up at least half now and the rest no later than 24 hours from now right here."

Pender and I couldn't believe our good luck. We were thrilled to drive the cars before anybody else could, particularly those that were most likely in our budgets. On top of that, we were getting an outstanding rate of pay for a little more than a couple hours of "work." Things went well for the first 45 minutes, but my favorite car sold for $750, which was way over my budget. The one Pender had his eye on was eliminated when it looked like the radiator started overheating and smoking up. Tim yelled, "Roll the car, get it out of here before it blows up!"

Another car I wanted to bid on went for $575. The price started climbing between two people after I threw in a bid for $400. Unfortunately, every car Pender liked went for almost $1000.

I drove my third choice on the list about an hour and fifteen minutes into the show. It was a black '64 Plymouth Belvedere with a push button automatic transmission that had 78,000 miles on it. The interior was intact and very clean. There was no radio, but the heater worked. There were minor dents on the sides of the headlights, but no rust. As I drove it up, I purposely stalled the engine twice. After someone bid $380, the auctioneer yelled "Going once, going twice," and I called out "$390!" The old guy dressed in the tan suit and checkered shirt, who had bid on several other cars, yelled, "$400!"

"$410," I bid.

"$420," he bid.

"$430," I hollered.

"$440," he responded.

"$450," I countered.

The old guy just smiled and shook his head.

Tim quickly said into the microphone, "Going once, going twice, it's yours" and pointed to me. "Roll the car, get it out of here!"

I had my first car! Pender came up empty. Tim thanked us after it was over and gave us $50 each in cash, telling us that we did a good job. I gave it back to him with $250 out of my wallet, and he said, "Be here with the balance by no later than noon tomorrow and it's yours. If you don't come up with the money by then, we keep the car and you forfeit the deposit." We thanked him. I thanked Pender for his help. I was on cloud nine riding home.

The next day, Pender drove me out there and right at noon I paid off the remainder of what I owed, filled out the paperwork, got the temporary registration and keys and shook hands with Tim. I noticed the old guy with the checkered shirt and sport coat from yesterday was hanging around. I was about to go over and ask him if he bought a car that someone didn't show up and pay for, but Pender grabbed me by the arm and said, "Forget it – that guy was a shill for the auctioneer. He was bidding to drive up the prices. He did that for a couple of cars I drove. They know the least amount they're worth."

For two weeks I was driving around the area with the license plate *2249AD*. I liked the numbers 22 and 49, so I thought that could be good luck. There seemed to be no problems at all with the car, but The lack of a radio was annoying. However, I was told by Francis, a guy I knew who was working at a local gas station, "You got a slant 6 engine and it purrs like a kitten." A few minutes after he opened up the hood to check it out, he sold me a new gas cap. My friend Van, who knew a lot more about cars than I did, thought I got a good deal – his father had just traded in a '64 Chrysler with a push-button transmission. He chuckled when I christened the car, "The Lambmobile."

A week after Labor Day, the Lambmobile and I were off to Pittsburgh with a planned stopover in Rochester to spend the night with relatives there. I had never driven that far before – certainly no more than about 30 miles on the New York State Thruway. Thankfully, it was a 75-degree, sunny day. With no radio in the car, I rolled down all the windows and sang as many songs as I remembered from the jukebox in my head, to ensure that I wouldn't doze off at the wheel. Just as I hit the first I-90 Exit for Rochester, I heard a loud *"bla-bada blabada"* noise coming from the rear of my car. I thought, *"Oh, shit – I wonder if that's the muffler or tail pipe. Something is definitely wrong."* Luckily, I made it to a Monro Muffler shop about 10 miles away. *I thought, "Good thing I'm staying at my uncle's instead of a motel. This is gonna cost me some bucks."* All the mechanics seemed busy as I drove into the place, and the guy at the service desk told me to stay in the waiting room after I described the awful sound coming from underneath the car. He told me that it would be about an hour before they could get to it, but it sounded like a bad muffler. Later on, I went out to observe what they were doing and the mechanic working on my car said that the muffler had a hole in it from rusting out. As I started to walk away, he also remarked, "Hey, kid – your shocks are gone. You want them taken care of, don't you?"

I responded, "Yeah, go ahead and put them in. I don't want the car to fall apart if go over a bump or a hole in the road."

"Dammit," I thought. As I sat in the small waiting room, I calculated about how much this would cut into my finances for landing a decent apartment when I got to Pittsburgh. At least it was my last semester in college and I had enough for tuition, but I would have to work part-time again almost as soon as I moved into my new place. My boss at the shoe store would hire me back, but if that didn't happen, maybe I could work at the state liquor store downtown. My buddy Mort, in a letter to me just before I left, said that they hired one of our friends he had recently encountered while he was on campus.

I thanked my aunt, uncle and cousins for their hospitality and left their house bright and early the next morning on my journey to Pittsburgh, filling up the tank right after I left their house. Gas was about 30 cents a gallon, and I was getting roughly a surprising 25 miles per gallon on the Interstate. I zoomed down I-90 with varying degrees of traffic – sludging through Buffalo, cruising through a smooth part of the trip to the Pennsylvania state line, eating lunch at a fast-food joint in Erie, and proceeding mostly "stop and go" down U.S. 19 where I gassed up again near Grove City. Just as I was hitting the afternoon rush hour traffic time in Pittsburgh, I pulled over to a phone booth and called Don, my ex-college roommate, who invited me to stay at his apartment for the night. I was tired, but I got a copy of the Pittsburgh Press and mapped out a strategy for checking out any dwelling for rent in the Shadyside or Oakland sections of town where I could move in immediately. Don was like my friend Van from back home, an excellent amateur mechanic, and he gave his initial assessment of the Lambmobile. We talked as I let him drive it for a couple of miles early in the evening.

"It seems OK. You made this long trip all right. I love the slant 6 engine. How can you stand it without a radio?"

"Good thing we had your stereo on all the time in the two years we lived together in the dorm, and I stored all those songs from the past 10 to 15 years in my mind. Too bad I didn't have the same memory for all the material in the courses I took when we lived together."

"But you're doing better now – what's another extra semester?"

"You're right. It's a little embarrassing that I didn't graduate with you guys several months ago. However, that's the price I pay for switching my major several times in '66. But my grades will keep getting higher and I probably would've been on my way to Vietnam by now. I read your letter – you had a good time in Europe again for the summer and you landed a job teaching. You got it made. They can't draft you. I'm hoping to go to grad school in February if any place accepts me. How's the *'White Elephant'* (his 1948 Packard) running?"

"As good as ever" he replied. "My brother and I may be getting a '46 Packard that we'll store at my dad's house in Fairbank. You ought to get a few years out of your car. Just keep checking the fluids. Getting the oil changed every 5000 miles for an old car and keeping anti-freeze in it are the best things you can do for a car."

The next day, I found a decent small apartment that I could move into that night on the edge of Shadyside – the coolest section in town for anyone in their 20's to live. The day after that I arranged to get a phone hooked up, and I drove to school to register for the upcoming semester. "This sure beats taking the bus," I thought. My classes would start on the following Monday. I parked my car at a street near the campus, and after registration, I walked downtown to the shoe store where I worked from January until June. Mrs. D., the manager, hired me back, but not for quite as many hours as I had hoped because she just hired some young chick to work part-time also. I negotiated with her for at least 12 hours a week instead of 20, but at least I was starting on Saturday, and I knew I was a good shoe salesman.

I sauntered back to where I parked and got the first of what was to be a slew of tickets accumulated over the coming months. Just as I was about to get into the car, another ex-roommate of mine from my junior year was walking down the street and I called over to him. "Hey, Will, check out my new second-hand wheels!"

Will was from downstate New York. Like Don, he was a car aficionado, and he was all smiles as he trotted over to me. After making quick small talk about how I got the car at a state auction, and my new muffler and shocks, he said, "Cool! Can I drive it a little? I never drove a car with a push button transmission before."

I gave him the keys and we drove it up Forbes Avenue. After about a mile, he said, "Hey, your oil pressure light is flashing. That could be a problem. We went back toward the campus, pulled into a parking lot and he checked the oil. "It's not down any at all, but you better have it looked at. Other than that, your car rides and sounds pretty nice."

"Thanks for warning me about another unexpected pain in the ass coming, Will", I said. I'll get it looked at right away."

I drove him back to his car and stopped into a gas station near my new apartment. I was told to bring it in the next morning. I arrived at the Boron service station at 7:30 a.m. The mechanic told me that he would have to drain out all the oil, clean the pan, put in 5 quarts of new 10/30 oil, a new oil filter and air cleaner, see if the pumps were all working OK, check the plugs and points to see if it needed a tune up, give it a lube job and take it for a test run, and the whole thing would take a few hours. He cautioned me that at worst, it could be the beginning of major engine trouble, at best, just an irritating electrical problem.

"Better safe than sorry," I thought. I was living 3 blocks away, so I told him I'd come back around noon because I was getting a phone hooked up that morning. Anyway, I didn't want to camp out in that dinky little waiting area with nothing to read but *Car and Driver*, *Outdoor Life*, *Field and Stream* and some gun magazine. There were no publications about the Pirates, Steelers, or Penguins, or the local paper there, from what I noticed.

At 11 o'clock, the phone company guy hooked up all the wires and gave me a new lime colored phone – the first color phone I ever had. As soon as the technician got through, I went back to the gas station just as my car was being parked into their lot about 20 yards away from the gas pumps. The mechanic motioned me into the office where he said, "Well, there's good news. There's nothing wrong with the oil pump or the engine, you're not leaking oil anywhere, and it doesn't really need a tune up. So, it's got to be a short in the light. You would have to go to a dealer for electrical problems – we don't do that here. Or you could just let it go, because it probably isn't that serious of a problem."

"That's a relief" I said. "What do I owe you?""

"$89 dollars, counting the parts and labor."

I muttered, as I drove away, "Son of a bitch, I think I got soaked. There goes a whole week's paycheck and more. I'm gonna have to buy dirt cheap food – Chef Boyardee in cans, TV dinners, a big loaf of white bread, and eggs to last me the next 10 days. No going out to bars or anything like that. Just go to work, to school, listen to the radio, and study. I'll have to be a hermit for the rest of the month."

I never did anything about the occasional flashing light. But as insurance for more things going wrong, I got a part-time job to start in late October through the end of the year at a state liquor store downtown. I estimated that it would pay more than selling shoes; Mrs. D. told me she would be cutting me back to working Saturdays only on November 1st, anyway. At the liquor store I was mostly helping to unload trucks and stock shelves, in addition to working behind the counter. My calculations were correct – that job actually paid better per week than selling shoes, even though I didn't work many more hours per week than at the shoe store.

The next several months were uneventful for the well-behaved Lambmobile. Right after the first of the year there were a couple of minor Lambmobile events. I had a date with an attractive girl I met at the university library, but once she got into the car, she asked me to turn on the radio.

I said, "It's good that I don't have one – we can talk and get to know each other better."

She said, rolling her eyes, "That's weird. You know, I've never been in a car like this before. There's no radio? You have to push buttons after you turn on the engine?"

Instead of going to a movie, she suggested, "Why don't we have a drink at one of the bars in Shadyside?"

Shadyside was a section of Pittsburgh with a lot of bars, restaurants, and night clubs filled with young people. I said, "Sure." I was thinking, "This could be even better."

After one drink she said she had to go home because of something she forgot that she had to do very early the next morning. She didn't even give me a quick kiss goodnight at her door.

"It's got to be the Lambmobile, I can't be me," I thought. I saw her at the library about 5 days later and asked her out again, but she shot me down. I decided that maybe she's nice on the surface, but she's nothing but a damn snob underneath.

A week later I backed into a Cadillac in a store parking lot. The guy had just come in behind me and parked – I didn't notice him. I slammed on the brakes quick. I got a small dent in my fender; the Cadillac didn't even get a scratch. He was nice about it and told me to forget the whole thing because the Cadillac wasn't damaged, and we didn't need to call the police or insurance companies. I happily obliged. It was the first time I'd ever been in any kind of accident driving a car.

Right after I got my degree in late January, I got a temporary job with the Pittsburgh Penguins NHL hockey team doing promotions and sales by telephone soliciting and delivering blocks of tickets for certain "nights" of the season (e.g., Ladies' Night; Kids' Night – where you could win a pony in a raffle, etc.). The office was not at the Civic Arena, but in a hotel downtown, for some reason. One benefit was they gave us free tickets to certain selected Penguins games – blue line seats, about 15 rows up at the Civic Arena. But because I just graduated from college, my military draft classification changed to 1-A with the notification in the mail right after celebrating my grades for the semester. My days in Pittsburgh were numbered.

I was at the Penguins-Chicago Blackhawks game on the night of February 27th. I felt like having a beer after the game, so I went out to one of the bars in Shadyside for a nightcap and I ran into Gus, a 3rd year law student from Pitt that I knew. Gus was a close friend of Frank, the guy who lived next door to me last year. Frank was a graduate student at the Art Institute of Pittsburgh. Their friend

Asok, who was graduating from the Art Institute tomorrow and going back to India on Monday, was with him.

As we had a drink together, Gus said, "There's a going away party in Shadyside on Saturday night for Asok at a female student's apartment. Her name is Theresa. Your old next door neighbor Frank will be there."

Asok said, "Would you like to come?"

"Sure, I'll be there, I said."

"Gus gave me the name of the girl and the Highland Avenue address and said, "It starts about 8:30, or 9 o'clock – BYOB. I'll tell Frank that you'll be there."

"Great. I won't feel like I'm totally crashing it then. I'll bring a 6-pack, is that OK?"

"Sure. Most of us will be drinking wine and eating cheese. I'm bringing a fifth of Jim Beam It'll be good to have some beer for anyone who wants that."

"This might be the last party I go to in this town," I thought.

Indeed, it turned out to be my last party in Pittsburgh, or anywhere else until the end of the year. Saturday night, I revved up the Lambmobile and parked near Theresa's apartment just before 9 p.m. About 15 people were already there, and more kept arriving over the next few hours. Frank was there, and so were Gus and Asok, but except for Frank, I didn't get much of a chance to talk to any of them. At 10:30, Frank asked to borrow the Lambmobile to take a close friend of his, Sylvia, home because she wasn't feeling well, and he said he'd be back in about 45 minutes. True to his word, Frank came back at 11:15. In the meantime, I was starting to feel no pain from drinking beer, wine, and doing some heavy flirting with a couple of girls. By about 1:15 I was definitely drunk, and I had to get out of there, even though the party was still going strong. I went downstairs to get my coat at the bottom of the stairs and a cute girl was passed out in the pile of coats right on top of mine. I woke her up and she started going at it hot and heavy with me. After 10 minutes, I said, "C'mon, let's get out of here and I'll drive you to my place and we can continue this. What's your name?"

"Kathy."

"Kathy, let's get our coats and go to my car."

I got about 20 yards up the street and suddenly I panicked, thinking, "Where the hell is the Lambmobile? Where did Frank park it? Whoa – I don't even have my keys. I hope some bastard didn't steal it."

I grabbed Kathy's hand and excitedly exclaimed, "We got to go back to the party!" I hoped Frank was still there.

People were coming out of Theresa's, and you could hear the loud din of voices from upstairs. Just as Kathy and I were outside of the entrance, some asshole threw a flower pot out the window and it bounced off a police car that happened to be cruising by. The cops grabbed me, Kathy, and a few other people and jammed us into the cop car, taking us to the East Liberty police station. As we were about two blocks away from the party, I saw what I thought was the Lambmobile and yelled, "Hey, there's my car – somebody must've stolen it – let me out!"

The cops laughed. But they didn't laugh when I said a few minutes later, "Don't worry, they'll just take our names and let us go," as I started to make out with Kathy.

The cop who was driving firmly told me to "cut it out!"

I said to her as they led us all into the police station, "I think I got a 'Get Out Of Jail Free' card from a Monopoly game in my wallet."

The other cop didn't like that remark at all. As we waited a few minutes, they let everybody go except me and Kathy and led us off to separate areas. Mine was a solo cell with a big 7-foot-long metal slab and an open toilet that didn't flush. After realizing, "Wow, these bars are real," I passed out and went to sleep.

At 7 a.m., they got me up and offered me a 16-ounce paper cup of warm water, telling me that I was going downtown in a few minutes. I was hung over and was trying to prepare some kind of defense, but thinking over and over, "Where's the Lambmobile? Where's my car?" A few minutes later, two guards loaded me into a paddy wagon, and we sped off to the Allegheny County jail downtown – a place I had walked by many times when I was in college. They dumped me into a cell that had about 20 guys in it. Some of the tougher dudes asked people what they were in for. A 16-year-old kid was picked up for "loitering," which pissed off some of the guys that cops would dump him in here for that. Two guys around 20 or so got nailed for burglary, and they were joking that it would get them out of the draft. When two of the guys came over to me to find out about what I had done, I bullshitted to them, "I was at a party, I was picking up this girl, and when I went outside the place some prick must've stolen my car. I got pissed, and just as I started yelling, cops drove by and pulled us into their car."

At that moment a guard came by, called out my name and led me out to the courtroom. Just before I got in there, I saw Kathy, who smiled at me and started to get tearful. An older man, probably her father, yelled, "There's the son of a bitch," as he tried to fight through the cops to get at me. They put us in separate areas of the courtroom.

There were a couple of cases before ours. The first guy shrugged it off as he was led away; I didn't know what his charges were. The next guy was being held for assault with a deadly weapon; but apparently, he used a board with nails in it, not a gun or a knife. He must have had a prior record because the judge gave him a 7-year sentence, and the thug was screaming at the judge that he would get his revenge on him when he got out of jail. The judge was obviously angry. Then the bailiff called me and Kathy up to the stand to be sworn in. The charges were read, "Public Intoxication, Disorderly Conduct, Contributing to The Delinquency of a Minor, and Resisting Arrest. How do you plead?"

I was shocked, and just as I was about to say, "Not Guilty" and request a Public Defender, Kathy cried, "Guilty! Your honor – the whole thing is true!" And she started to cry.

I shockingly said to her, "What? How old are you?"

"19," as she sobbed.

"Your Honor, I'll admit I was intoxicated, but I didn't think I was disorderly, and I didn't resist arrest."

The cop then mentioned about my cuddling with her in the police car, yelling about the Lambmobile, and smart-ass remarks I made. The judge asked me about my employment. I told him I was employed by the Pittsburgh Penguins (I didn't tell him it was a part-time temporary job, and I didn't work inside at the Civic Arena).

The judge then asked me, "Did you play hockey?"

I said, "I used to play hockey, Your Honor." I didn't tell him it was as an amateur in upstate New York and almost all of it was on ponds. I then told him that we were just walking right outside of the house where the party was to find my car when the police came, and I didn't resist going into the car. The judge, begrudgingly, said that he would drop all the charges except Public Intoxication, declared that we would each have to pay a $50 fine and that he never wanted to see us in his court again, and he pounded his gavel declaring the case over.

Just then, Gus came rushing in, yelling, "Your honor, your honor – these are my clients!"

"You're too late," the judge forcefully declared. "Next case."

The girl's parents whisked her away while her father growled at me one last time. An old social worker grabbed me and said it was part of the court proceeding that she had to ask me if I wanted spiritual counseling and help for my alcoholism. I told her that I just had to find my car because I thought somebody had stolen it, and after last night the police wouldn't be of any help. She said, I had to sign that I declined that option, and I told Gus, "Please get me out of here now!"

I had $35, and Gus paid the balance of the fine. He led me out to the side entrance, and several people who were at the party clapped and cheered briefly, saying, "How does it feel to be a free man? How does it feel to be out of jail?"

"I just got to get to my car, wherever the hell it is," I replied. "Hey, where are my keys?"

Gus said, "I got 'em. Somehow, they must've fallen out of your pants pocket before the cops threw you into their car. Frank went outside as they drove away, and he found them. He gave them to me this morning. By the way, you were so drunk you took the wrong coat. You ought to go to Theresa's and pick yours up."

"Where's my car? Where's the Lambmobile?"

"Frank couldn't find a place to park, so he parked it a few blocks away. You don't remember?"

"No, just get me home and I'll walk over to Theresa's this afternoon. I just want to go home and get a few hours of sleep."

Later, I took a long walk to Theresa's place. She was home, and said she never dreamed the party would swell to such a crowd and get rowdy. The party broke up right after the cops came. Nobody admitted to throwing the flower pot out the window, and she didn't know who did it, but the cops called another patrol car and took a couple more people in. She said the girl, Kathy, was at the party because she knew a few people that were being honored who were Art Institute of Pittsburgh graduates.

Theresa then shocked me saying, "She had never been to a party before where there was alcohol flowing. It was the first time in her life she had ever been drinking."

"Oh, God – no wonder her father wanted to kill me this morning!"

"By the way, here's your coat. That's George's you're wearing – he is coming by in a little while to get his."

"I got my keys from Gus, Frank's friend. Where's Frank, and where's my car? I thought I saw my car on the way to the police station."

"It's on Spahr Street, right off College Avenue – about 3 or 4 blocks away. I guess there were a lot of parties in Shadyside last night, and that was the only place Frank could get a spot to park. Frank is probably home. He said he'd call you tonight."

"Thanks, Theresa. I'm really sorry about everything that happened."

I left and made it to where the Lambmobile was parked. Someone had broken into the trunk and stolen my spare tire. The glove compartment was open, but nothing had been taken. I only had a pencil, some old parking tickets and a small pad of paper in there, anyway. I drove it home and talked to Frank later who told me I was drunk to the max, and I would've got nailed for a DWI if I had tried to drive it, anyway. He was in the bathroom inside when all hell broke loose. Frank didn't know who Kathy was or where she lived, so I never got a chance to apologize to her. Unfortunately, I never saw Frank or Gus again.

I moved out at 9 a.m. on April Fool's Day and drove back to my parents' house. About a half an hour after I left, I remembered that back in my apartment I left a shoe box with some of my college papers, some sports mementos, and the letter from the draft board in New York ordering me to report for my draft physical in Albany on April 3rd. I went back to get the shoe box.

My landlady asked, "Are you in trouble? A policeman came by a few minutes ago and said you owe $130 worth of parking tickets. I thought you'd come back for this box."

"I don't have $130, and I doubt if I'll come back to Pittsburgh for years, after what happened a few weeks earlier. I'm not in any serious trouble, but it's a long story, and I don't have time to tell you about it. Thanks for keeping the shoe box."

It was a long, exhausting drive, and after I stopped to eat somewhere around Newburgh, New York. I discovered that my left rear tire had developed a slow leak, so periodically had to pull into gas stations to keep it filled with air. At that point, I went over to U.S. 9 because I was afraid that I might have a blowout in the tire on the NY State Thruway. I made it home at 11:30 that night with the tire totally flat as I pulled in outside my parents' house.

I passed the draft physical with flying colors, and I was supposed to be inducted into military service on May 16th, but on April 17th, after spending several days seeing all the recruiters, I decided to join the Army on delayed enlistment. I did this because I wouldn't have to report for active duty until September 9th, and I figured, "What's an extra year in the service? At least I'll get trained for something I want to do, instead of being an infantry grunt." I had no more problems with the Lambmobile and enjoyed driving it for the rest of the summer, and even for the rest of the year. My brother drove it around town on weekends when he was home from college in New Hampshire.

When I was home on leave from the Army at Christmastime, there was a slight sweet smell after I drove it a few miles one day. Van came over to check the Lambmobile and said, "Hey, your anti-freeze is leaking. You're lucky the radiator didn't smoke and blow up." He drained the radiator, put a can of Stop-Leak and antifreeze in it, got a new radiator cap for it, and when I drove it several hours later it ran fine. But during the times I drove it when I was home for several days in January before being sent to Vietnam, I had to blast up the heat as high as it would go for the temperature to be OK. The whole time I was in Vietnam, my brother drove it sparingly. Van was virtually "supervising" him by checking in with him periodically about the Lambmobile. According to Van, surprisingly, everything was fine with the Lambmobile the whole year I was in Vietnam, except that the heating core was shot.

I came home for the month of January 1971, and I was re-assigned to Germany. It was a wickedly cold month; I went from almost 100 degrees in Vietnam to 12 below zero in upstate NY. To help the car's engine start up the next morning, I usually either went over to see Van or else I spent brief times in bars until midnight, the night before. But every morning, the good old Lambmobile started up – even one morning when it was -28 degrees – and I swear I could hear other people on the block cursing at me because their new cars wouldn't kick over at 7:30 a.m. when I drove my mother to her job downtown.

A few nights before I was supposed to take off to my next duty station in Germany, I was out bar hopping. Coming home, I was definitely feeling no pain. About a mile away from home, a guy cut me off just before a light turned red at a corner and I slowly skidded into the rear end of his car. My front bumper was covered in snow and ice, as was his rear bumper. I thought, "Maybe the snow and ice didn't cause any dents for either of us. I hope he's not pissed." He got out of his car, as I did mine – we were both drunk.

"Doesn't look like there's any damage here," I slurred.

He bobbed his head and replied, "Yeah – don't call the cops."

I pulled out a note pad and a pen from my glove compartment, and we decided to scribble down our names and phone numbers to exchange, in case there were any dents or scratches. Since I was leaving the country soon and we were both drunk, I gave him a phony name and number. The next day I noticed there was a tiny dent in my right front bumper. While I was out at a store, I felt a little guilty about any damage I might've caused him that we didn't notice. I decided to call him from a phone booth on a whim. The lady who answered the phone said she knew of no such person or car. I laughed and felt relieved that there were no cops around at the scene last night. I reported to Ft. Dix, NJ a few days later, and was in Germany by the end of the week.

In May after responding to a letter asking how the Lambmobile was holding up, my mother informed me that my brother took the car to New Hampshire for a week last month and one night when he was out with friends, the car skidded on the ice, hit a tree, and had landed in the Contoocook River! I was pissed! I dashed off a letter to her saying that I knew that he was probably out partying with friends and that he should pay for the cost of the car. My mother wrote back that it was turning into a real piece of junk, anyway. Somehow, Van got it running and my mother wound up selling it for $50 to be put in a demolition derby! She wrote, "You'll get another car when you get out of the Army next year." I was furious, but I felt like I was a light year away from home and couldn't even get any leave to go back there until at least October. I wrote to Van, who responded to me in June – he said that he thought the engine was starting to run badly the last time he saw it in late March – and he was surprised it made it to New Hampshire.

"Requiescat In Pace, Lambmobile." I didn't get a chance to say goodbye.

CHAPTER 2

The Green Toad: 1972-1973

I got out of the Army a year later. In Europe I was used to either walking or taking trains everywhere, with an occasional taxi ride. That wouldn't cut it back in the USA unless I lived in New York City, so I had to buy some kind of car. No friends were left in the old neighborhood, but at least Van was living not far away in Schenectady for some advice if needed. I could borrow my mother's or father's car only several times before I couldn't stand it anymore. After about 6 weeks of being a civilian again, I started checking out ads in the local paper. There was a guy a few miles away who was selling a '68 green Ford Falcon 2 door sedan, 6-cylinder engine with a little under 65,000 miles on it for less than $1000. I called him right away and took it for a test drive with him. After 4 or 5 miles, everything seemed fine – tires and brakes were OK, as was making a U-turn, and using all the gears. The interior had no rips or big stains; the automatic transmission was tight; no flaking paint; no dents; just a couple of very minor rust spots on the outside. The lights, radio, heater, wipers and battery all were fine. I noticed a little bit of a hum, but no engine knocking. Nothing under the hood (the belts and hoses, etc.) looked abnormal, as far as I could tell. There was no manual in the glove compartment, but I could always write to

Ford to get one, if I needed it. I liked the car so much, I didn't even dicker much with the price he was asking. I paid him $875 in cash and drove it down to the Department of Motor Vehicles to register and put plates on it.

The next day I went to see Van in Schenectady, who thoroughly checked it over and drove it for several miles. He remarked, "Looks like you got a pretty good deal. I wonder why the guy let it go fairly cheap. Did he have any repair records?"

"Oh, no. I forgot to ask and there was nothing in the glove compartment. How could I be so damn dumb?"

"Looks like all it needs is an oil change and filter at the moment. That's easy to do on this car. I can show you how. At some point you might need a muffler, but that's all I can see."

"If I don't have to sink much money into it for a couple of years, that's OK with me. Too bad you got married. I want to go on a trip up to the Maritimes in Canada for a month right after the 4th of July. I really don't want to take my brother with me, but I had to invite him because I need somebody to help contribute to the expense of the trip, and he's willing to go. I'm having a hard time adjusting to America after being away for so long. Do you think the car can make it up there and back with no serious problems? I'd probably put about 2000 miles on it."

"I think the car should be OK for the trip. It's not like you're going out to California and back. We know Danny and you may start fighting, but I hope it's fun for you, otherwise."

There were two other reasons I wanted to go to Canada. First, I missed traveling in Europe, like I did most weekends when I lived there. Second, it was raining almost every damn day in June, and it looked like there was much better weather way up north and to the east. Plus, there was going to be a total eclipse of the sun in July in Nova Scotia, which would be cool to see. I figured I probably wouldn't put more than about 1500 miles on the car; 2000 at most. I didn't start school until September in Massachusetts. "Might as well have one last great summer before I have to get serious about my life," I thought.

Danny and I took off for Canada on July 5th. We planned to stay every two nights sleeping in the car – one of us sleeping in the front bench seat, one of us sleeping in the back seat, and then one night together in a cheap motel. This was OK for the first few days, through Maine and into New Brunswick. Then we started fighting about where to go, what to do, where to eat, and how we would be dressed going out at night. We took turns driving. While we were cruising down the roads, we didn't take any naps because we didn't trust each other about which roads to take and where to stay. In Saint John, as we pulled into the Fundy Line motel parking lot, I got a scare. The engine started missing a little and it stalled and didn't start up right away. It turned out that the choke was stuck and I had to put a pencil in it for a minute to keep it running and idling well. I had to do this intermittently in the morning for the next couple of weeks. At Shediac, we pulled off onto the side of a dirt road near the beach to spend the night. At 3 a.m. a couple of guys were hovering around the car.

One asked, "What the hell is this thing doing here with New York plates? Hey – somebody's inside – two of them!"

I took my knife out of my pocket and thought, "Oh, shit. This could be big trouble."

The other guy saw me and said, "We better get the hell out of here – they're alive and they're waking up!"

They ran away, thankfully. We took off for Prince Edward Island as the sun came up. But despite that scare, sleeping in the car had not been too uncomfortable and nobody bothered us again.

A few nights later, as it got very dark, we were about 15 miles outside of New Glasgow, Nova Scotia and I heard a familiar *"thump, thump, thump"* coming from the rear of the vehicle.

Danny yelled, "What the hell is that?"

"It's a flat tire" I said. You ever change one before?"

"No. I called AAA once."

"Well, I'm gonna need your help. Shit, we're out in the middle of nowhere and it's dark as hell. I gotta find a fairly flat place off the side of the road if I can."

I put my flashers on and drove about 20 m.ph. for about a ¼ of a mile before I found a very small clearing right next to high bushes. It was the left rear tire. Fortunately, I had a good spare in the trunk that was on a wheel. My flashlight worked OK. We pulled all our baggage, dirty clothes, etc. out and threw them into the back seat. As soon as we did this, about 1000 mosquitoes, who apparently hadn't eaten all day, descended on us for their dinner.

"Hold the flashlight while I get the jack in position with the half-ass lug wrench." I yelled.

"Christ, I'm getting eaten alive!"

"Son of a bitch! These tiny bastards are finding every single nook and cranny of our bodies."

"Hurry up, dammit, or I'm gonna turn off the flashlight. Ow! These fucking things won't stop!"

"No, don't turn off the light. I can't see a goddamn thing without it – it's pitch black out here! I'm trying to get this tire on as fast as I can. Ooh! Ah!"

The bitching at each other went on for 20 minutes before the tire was in place. We got to a gas station shortly before they were closing and the guy agreed to plug the tire for us, but he said we had to buy a full tank of gas first. The other part of the deal was that I gave him $10 to let us stay in my car in his little parking lot out back. We didn't get that much sleep because we scratched ourselves all night long. The next day after sunrise, we drove all over the spectacular Cabot Trail and pulled into a Holiday Inn in Sydney for an early check-in at 1:30 p.m.

"I really want to take a dip in the pool, take a shower, check out the total eclipse of the sun, and rest up for dinner someplace," I said.

As we got out of the car, Danny remarked, "We can't use the pool. Of all the freakin' days – they picked this one to paint the pool!"

We checked in, anyway, and we hopped in our beds to take a brief nap. We didn't wake up until 6 p.m. I turned on the TV for any local, national or international news. Then came the lead story.

I cried, "I don't believe this shit! We missed the total eclipse of the sun this afternoon!"

"That's one of the reasons we came to Nova Scotia in the first place," Danny grumbled.

Over the next several days everything was fine with the car, but not with Danny and me. We started fighting over trivial things.

"I want to go to Newfoundland," he kept saying.

"We can't go to Newfoundland. We don't have enough money to make it there and back."

"Yes, we do. Even if we don't, we could get cheap jobs for a week, quit, and go home. We may never get this chance again."

"If the car breaks down in 100 miles or more of nothingness, we're screwed. We already had one close call."

"We don't have anything to do for the next few weeks. Don't be a prick."

"You're the one who's a prick. All you do is bitch about where to stay, where to eat, what bars to go out to, and you're smoking a pack a day in the car. We could've picked up those two girls hitchhiking to Prince Edward Island the other day while you were driving, but you just whizzed right by and ignored them. In fact, I'm driving from now on."

"If we can't go to Newfoundland, we're going to Clam Harbour Beach and we're going swimming in the ocean. You promised me we'd do that. It's a beautiful day."

We went to Clam Harbour Beach and there was nobody there. It was about 75 degrees and sunny. I got in the water and started to swim.

"*Aaaah!* This is the coldest water I've ever been in," I yelled. I lasted about one minute before I got out of there. He stayed in the ocean for about 5 or 10 minutes, laughing. As Danny came out of the water, we asked a guy walking by if he knew what the water temperature was.

"11°."

"That's on the Metric system you have now, I said. "What is it Fahrenheit?"

"About 54°."

"Thanks. That's why nobody else is swimming here, I guess."

"If you want to go swimming, then go to the north beaches of Prince Edward Island or go to New Brunswick," he said, as he walked away.

"Danny, let's get out of here. How the hell could you stand it?"

He just started laughing. After we dried off, we both agreed that we were not getting along on this trip, and we had enough of each other. I took him to Halifax the next day and he was able to get on a stand-by flight. He flew home.

A couple days later, I was driving into Truro and a brief thunderstorm came up. My windshield wipers and radio both conked out. I thought, "No! My battery's dying!"

I pulled over to the side of the road for about 20 minutes and left the engine running. The car limped into a gas station just inside the city limits. After about 20 minutes, the teenage mechanic couldn't figure out what was wrong with it.

"It's not your battery. It's probably some electrical problem. You can go over to the Ford dealership a few blocks away."

My poor Ford Falcon sputtered over there. It was a small dealership and a slow day for the service department. The mechanic got me in right away.

"Looks like the ignition switch is burning out. It's amazing you had power enough to start the car. We've had this problem with '68 Falcons. I see you're from New York. Where'd you buy this car – Montreal?"

"No. I live about 200 miles away from Montreal. I'm the second owner, I think. I bought it from a guy who lives a few miles away from me. Why do you ask?"

"I guess you didn't know this, then, but you have a Canadian Ford Falcon. It was born and raised in our factory in Ontario."

"Wow! That's a good thing, then?"

"Sure is – I know all about the '68 Falcons, and I can probably help you more with your particular car than anyone in New York."

"Looks like it's actually my lucky day," I said, with a smile.

He grinned back and replied, "This'll hold the cost of the labor down, eh?"

The job was done quickly. Nobody else came in, so when we were at the cash register, he started talking about baseball.

He said, "I'm a lifelong Dodgers fan. You know we had their AAA team here in the International League for years."

"Yeah. I remember that. All those great Dodger players in the 50s through the mid-60s came up in the ranks through Montreal. I like the Expos. I can get the games in French at night on my radio back home."

We talked about baseball for almost half an hour. He told me about the radio station where I could get the Montreal Expos games while I was driving in Nova Scotia, and I thanked him for that. I thanked him more profusely when he showed me the bill – only $26! I was thinking it would be twice that much. In my excitement after I drove away, I was near the Prince Edward Island ferry when

I thought, "Dammit! I forgot to ask him about the carburetor and the choke." But I didn't have any problems with them for the rest of the trip.

Things were fine all through the several days I was in Prince Edward Island. The guy at Clam Harbour was right about their beaches having warmer water. I noticed that driving in Prince Edward Island at night was very dark on the streets and particularly outside of any city areas, so I drove no faster than 35-40 m.p.h. The day I left Prince Edward Island, I sauntered into Fredericton, New Brunswick. Just as I pulled into a motel there, I noticed that my left front headlight and directional light both burned out. I said to no one, "Aw shit! Another uncomfortable night in a Holiday Inn parking lot to save money for what I would have to spend to fix them." I had to get them fixed, though, because I didn't want to get stopped by the RCMP or the cops in Maine (where I was headed the next day). I went to an auto parts store the next morning.

The guy behind the counter said, "There's a gas station down the street where you can get them put in cheap."

When I went to where he suggested, after the guy put in the lights for me, I asked about the electrical system in the car and the choke (remembering that I should've asked the guy in Truro at the dealership about them).

He said, "The electrical system is probably OK. I'm gonna give a quick spray into your choke and carburetor with some stuff I got." He removed the little pencil I had to hold the choke open, smiled, and remarked to me, "Whatever works, eh?"

I didn't ask what the spray stuff was, but he demonstrated the improvement in the choke and carburetor to me. He smiled again and said, "You want the pencil back that you stuck in your carburetor?"

"Just in case," I laughed.

I shelled out another $50 and I was on my way back to the U.S.A.

For the rest of the trip everything was fine with the car. I drove through Maine and northern New Hampshire; then to northern Vermont; then to Plattsburgh NY. I went up to Montreal but couldn't find a place to park or a cheap motel that had a vacancy, so I wound up in a flophouse in downtown Ottawa. At least they had a parking lot. That night, I thought about going to Toronto with a couple of ladies I met in a bar – they said they wanted to look for work there - but I had to ditch them when I realized I might not have enough money to make it back home. I returned to Montreal the next day because it was a chance to see a major league baseball game for the first time in 4 years. I had just enough money to do that, to check into a cheap motel, and afterwards to have a couple of beers and dance at a discotheque. As it turned out, that night, I met a lady named Celine – she was to be my long-distance girlfriend for the next 18 months. I cruised home smiling amid the gorgeous summer weather, almost flat broke. But it was worth it all, in spite of the aggravations with the car, which now seemed minor.

Six weeks later, I was living in Massachusetts, back in school again. Celine came down to see me in mid-October for an instant replay of our weekend rendezvous in Lake George in late August. The day after she left, I ran over a nail somewhere and the next morning my right rear tire was flat. "Just my shit luck," I thought. I didn't have enough money to get any new tires, so I put the spare on (which already had a plug in it) after I changed it and drove to the nearest gas station to get the damaged tire plugged.

The man said, "We got a sale on used tires, and there's some that will fit your car. $10 for recaps and $20 for retreads."

"That sounds like a good deal, but no thanks. I'll hang in there for a few weeks until I can buy some new tires," I lied.

"It looks like you might need new front tires in a little while. Sure you don't want to buy the recaps or retreads? The sale only lasts until tomorrow."

"No. I'm good," I replied.

To me, the front tires looked fine. When I got home, I put a quarter in the treads, and I could see the tip of Washington's head obscuring the "LIBERTY" on the quarter. The guy was bullshitting; the tires could last at least another 10,000 miles, I figured.

Three days later I was coming back from a grocery store when a block away from my apartment I started hearing the familiar *"whump whump"* and the car was pulling to the left. I parked it in a nearby driveway where nobody was home, and I was pissed when I saw that the left front tire was flat. I yelled out to nobody, "Jesus Christ! What evil things did I do to deserve this shit?"

The flat that had a hole filled with jagged glass in it and I changed it with the spare I had in the trunk. I'd be damned if I would go back to the same gas station where the guy was selling the retreads and recaps. Van told me once never to trust a recap, and a retread might blow out at any time. I got the tire plugged at another gas station in town and I was now driving on two plugged tires and a plugged spare. I toughed it out until Thanksgiving. When I was home during that long weekend, I was able to afford a couple of Firestone tires. Van, who was working at a gas station part-time, was able to mount and balance them for me.

Then the cold weather seemed to be taking a toll on my car. Right after Christmas, especially on cold mornings, it took a long time to warm up. It got so, coincidentally, if I felt good, the car ran well. If I felt like crap, the car ran the same way. Half the time I seemed not to be getting good gas mileage and, when the temperature was below freezing, it seemed like it was running on 5 cylinders. Thus, I decided to give it the nickname "The Green Toad" because of how it was hopping along. I had more problems with the choke again, so one weekend I went home and took it to a garage run by an old guy who lived around the corner from my parents.

My neighbor said, "I can't get to it for a few days. What you really need is a new carburetor."

"Joe, I can't afford to shell out $300 for that."

That Tuesday afternoon Joe adjusted the choke as well as he could and sold me a new air filter, which was within my budget. He also suggested a tune-up, but Van had said he could do that for me in his father's driveway in his spare time – I'd just have to buy the sparkplugs. I left the car with Van while I took my mother's '66

Chevy Impala convertible back to Massachusetts. We agreed that I'd bring it back home Friday night.

Thursday night we had a 6-inch snowstorm. I woke up at 7 a.m. and looked out the window to see how much snow was on my mother's car, parked across the street. Only it wasn't there. Just an empty parking space. I screamed, "What the fuck?" This woke up my roommate, Buck.

"I was frantic and asked him, "Hey, Buck, what time did you get in from work last night? My mother's car is gone! Did you notice it there when you got in?"

He groggily responded, "Yeah, I'm pretty sure I did see it. I came in at 12:30 from work, and you acknowledged that I got in and went right back to sleep. I didn't even give the car a second thought. Did somebody rip it off?"

"Yeah – it's not there! You think I'm pissed? Wait till I tell my mother! She's only had the car for a couple of months."

"This whole region from Springfield to Boston is the car theft area of New England – you locked it, didn't you?"

"Damn right I did!"

"Call the police."

I called the police station and because it wasn't an emergency, I was put on hold for 20 minutes before I slammed down the phone, put on my clothes, and coat and told Buck, "I'm going downtown to the police station and talk to them in person."

"Good luck. Unfortunately, I bet they don't do anything. They're more interested in hanging peoples' asses for unpaid parking tickets."

Buck was right. When I got to speak to the cop at the desk, he asked for all the details, and made a remark that this was the third car stolen overnight, and that cars from New York were "sitting ducks," and that whoever stole it probably took it to a makeshift chop shop somewhere in Boston to sell it for parts.

"These guys who steal cars are real pros, kid. Nobody's gonna steal a car in a snowstorm unless they really want it. We'll check into it and call you if we find out anything. Sorry I can't be of more help."

I never heard anything from the police. The next day, after taking a series of buses to get back to my parents' home, my whole family was angry.

My mother cried, "How could you let that happen? Now I have to get another car and my insurance doesn't cover stolen cars."

My brother chimed in, "Admit it – you had that car stolen, you shithead!"

My father bellowed, "Your car's outside. Get your ass back to Worcester first thing in the morning."

"I'm going to Van's. I'll be back tonight," I replied.

I called Van and told him my tale of woe. He told me to come over – his wife was at her parents' house and she was going out to play bingo later. We split a pizza and a 6 pack that I bought while he recorded a bunch of music in his den.

"At least your Green Toad is running OK now. I bought the plugs and tuned it up for you. You don't owe me anything. You're screwed – I feel sorry for you."

"Thanks a lot, Van. I don't know what I'd do without you."

The Green Toad was behaving much better through the spring. Celine came down and spent a 5-day weekend – fortunately, the Green Toad ran like a kitten. However, in mid-June it was running rough again. I drove it home for a weekend and Van drove it for a little while.

"Something's not right – it's like you're running on 5 cylinders again. Let's take a deeper look," he said, as we were in the driveway in his parents' house, which was only about a half mile away from my parents' home.

After fooling around under the hood for a while, he told me, "Start it up."

He probed the guts of the car with a flashlight, and said, "I hear a pinging noise. Rev the engine. I'm gonna look in back of the car. Then shut it off."

After I followed his instructions, he said, "The good news is that you didn't blow a valve gasket, but you got a tiny bit of oil around the cover. There's no blue smoke coming out the exhaust; otherwise, you'd really be screwed. I think you need a new head – the valve cover."

"Sounds like I am screwed, anyway."

"It could be a hell of a lot worse. I can take it out and put one in for you, but we have to go to a junkyard now and get one cheap. If you went to a dealer, the job'd cost you your ass."

"So, I can't let this go any longer?"

"Hell, no. You don't want to run the risk of having this thing catch on fire on the Mass Turnpike or the Mohawk trail. Good thing you made it here in one piece."

"If we get one, how long would it take to put it in?"

"Probably a couple of hours or so to make sure everything's running OK."

"I got the time, if you got the time. Let's do it."

Luckily, the first junkyard we went to had one from a '68 Falcon. I bought the shiny red head. Van put it in when we got back to his parents' driveway (with me handing him the tools and shining the flashlight), and the Green Toad was back on the road in the early evening. The valves and pistons looked OK, he said. More money down the drain, but Van was invaluable to me again. Although I paid for the head, he didn't take any money for the labor. "I love doing stuff like this. You can buy us the pizza and beer."

I was hurting financially for much of the summer of '73 because I was between part-time jobs and put in a lot of effort into school-work. Also, my GI Bill checks didn't come for 3 months, but after I marched into Senator Kennedy's office in Boston to complain, within 2 weeks the full amount miraculously arrived in the mail. I was driving to my parents' home one Saturday morning on the Mass Turnpike when I heard a "POW!" and the Green Toad was wobbling near a bridge just outside of Springfield. As luck(?) would have it, I was right near a big level clearing area 20 yards from the end of the bridge. I put my flashers on and hobbled there, hoping I wouldn't get hit from behind, but I thanked God I was safe. If I went over the bridge, I would have zoomed down 100 feet to my death. As I got out of the car, I saw that the Firestone tire was almost half blown out – a humungous hole! The wheel wasn't damaged, though. I mounted the spare, even though the jack was a little shaky, and made it home. I called Van early that afternoon and told him what happened.

"Come over to the gas station later on. I'm working there tonight. You can buy a good spare tire here."

"How much will it cost?'

"$20, and I'll mount it on the wheel for you. As usual, you buy the pizza and the beer, and we'll go home and listen to some music I just recorded on my reel to reel."

In October, the shoe store where I was working in Worcester went out of business, which put a dent in my finances. Celine wanted me to come up to Montreal for her birthday, but if I did that, I'd be absolutely flat broke until my next GI Bill check came a couple weeks later. She was not very happy when I said I couldn't help her celebrate, but we agreed to see each other for New Years' Eve. I didn't know if the Green Toad could make it up to her place and back without something else happening to set me back financially. I wondered if our relationship was coming to an end, anyway.

A few nights later, I went to stop into a convenience store to see Frank, my friend from school who worked nights there. I took a left across the street to go into a parking space just vacated in front of the store, and *"BAM!"* A guy in an old Buick apparently gunned his engine and slammed into the right rear of my car, throwing me up against the steering wheel. He was 30ish, reeked of marijuana, and screamed, "Look what you did to my car, asshole!"

"You're the asshole!" I yelled back. "You saw me go into the parking space and you didn't even put on your brakes!"

The argument went back and forth for a couple of minutes and Frank came out and said he called the cops; a patrol car showed up right away. As soon as he got there, some guy got out of Mr. Pothead's Buick and ran away across a wooded area.

I said to the cop, excitedly, "Hey! Why is that bastard running away?"

He turned and saw him, but just then, two other cars were in a head on collision right near the intersection about 50 yards from the store. This distracted the cop, who said to me and Mr. Pothead, "You guys wait here."

Frank told me, "Park your car here and get in touch with some auto body shop to have it towed there in the morning."

"I have AAA, and I'll go with whoever they'd recommend. I'll call them ASAP."

The cop took down all the information from me and Mr. Pothead about 10 minutes later as another cop showed up to take care of the collision at the corner. Mr. Pothead's car was drivable, and he left angrily, not even taking any of my information. The dude had no insurance, either. I called Buck, who drove me to my place – we were not living together anymore, but we were still good friends, and he was off work that night.

Fighting off the whiplash I experienced the next morning, I called AAA, and they towed it to a nearby auto body shop. Ronnie, the guy who ran the place, said he'd take a look at it as soon as he could get to it. He called me 3 days later to come over to the garage.

"Your car's totaled because the frame is bent underneath, but I can take it for the parts. You could get it towed someplace else, and they might be able to get it running for you, but it'll never pass inspection anyway. You do owe me 3 days' worth of storage charges – $200."

"What? I can't afford that!"

"I got a '63 Plymouth Fury that I can sell you for $150. It runs OK, but you'd have to put a little work into it."

"No thanks, Ronnie. I wish I had known about any damn storage charges. I'll take my stuff out of the car (I didn't have much), you can have it, and I'll contact my insurance company today."

The Green Toad was gone to auto body heaven (or hell).

CHAPTER 3

The Vomit Comet: 1973-1975

I took connecting buses to my parents' home the next day. Although the incident with the Green Toad was bad luck, at least I didn't have any classes for the next 5 days. But there was good luck in store for me: I saw in the local newspaper that the next day that there was another auction for state cars in Albany at 1 p.m. at the same place where I bought the Lambmobile 5 years earlier. Van couldn't get off work, but Danny was out of college and unemployed – he drove me over to the grounds a half hour before the auction started. I didn't get a chance to look at every car, and this time they already had a couple of guys ready to drive the cars up front to the auctioneer, but I made a quick list of several cars that I could probably afford to bid on. Danny and I got seats on the bench in the front row of the bleachers not far from where the cars stopped when they were driven up to the auctioneer. I only had a little over $400 to spend this time, but I figured if I got some basic transportation for about 6 to 8 months, by that time I'd be out of school, have a decent paying job, and I could trade it in for something a lot better in the spring of '74.

At 1 o'clock, it was "Here we go again." Gibberish came from Tim the auctioneer's fast-talking voice interspersed with the bids from people and the familiar "Roll the car, get it out of here!" The first 20 minutes featured a parade of cars that I either didn't want or couldn't afford. Then my #1 choice, a '66 Mustang hardtop arrived. I quickly threw in a bid for $350 after the first guy bid $300. A few bids by other people later and it was gone. It went for $800. "I thought I'd at least try," I said to Danny.

A few cars later, a '69 Ford Maverick arrived. I bid $325 after the second bid. A couple bids later, I yelled out "$400!" But the bidding escalated, and it went for $650. 10 minutes later, a '68 Mercury Cougar arrived. I bid $325. Two more bids were placed, and I raised my hand to the auctioneer at $400 again. But for the third time I was left in the dust, and the car was sold for $500.

Danny said, "Looks like you're screwed."

I replied, "Jeez, I gotta get something. I can't go home empty handed."

Another 15 minutes passed before my 4th choice came on the scene – a '67 Mercury Comet. It was a black 4-door, 6-cylinder sedan that had an automatic transmission and an AM radio in it. The body had a couple of minor dents on it. I remembered it had about 80,000 miles on it and it was owned by the Department of Education. The right front tire was starting to go bald. The bidding started at $250. After $280, I started casting my lot. "$290," I said.

"$300," another guy raised.

"$310," I asserted.

"$320," another voice crowed.

"$330, I countered.

"$340," from the same voice.

"Uh, oh – a shill. Hope he doesn't go past $400."

"$350," I yelled.

Some more quick fast talk from the auctioneer, then, pointing to me, "Going once, going twice – you got it. Roll the car, get it out of here!"

"Looks like I pulled it out of my rear end," I said to Danny, smiling. The interior looked a little worn, but not bad. I agreed with Danny when he said it'd be a good idea to put newer front tires on the Comet ASAP. I paid in full for the car, and we went to the Motor Vehicle Department to get it registered with new plates, and afterwards I drove it to my parents' house. The next day there was an ad in the paper for a place near Albany that was selling tires dirt cheap. When the mechanic put the Comet up on the lift, he saw how uneven the right front was wearing and pounded the bottom of the tire with his hand.

"Oh, wow – you need ball joints."

"I thought a front-end alignment was all I'd need, at worst. Can I make a phone call real quick before you do anything?"

"Yeah. Use the pay phone outside."

I called Van and described the situation to him. He said, "If you don't have the ball joints replaced, you'd be taking a chance on having the car vibrating or veering off to one side."

"Bad luck again?"

"Yeah, but it's not that bad of a job. See if you can make a deal for the price of just the right front tire and the ball joints. Bring it over here after you're done. I want to see the car, anyway."

"I'll try. Thanks, Van."

The guy agreed to about $75 for the job, which left me with enough for a full tank of gas. I drove it over to Van's house and we took turns driving it for about 5 miles.

He said, "It runs pretty well. I hope it's OK in the cold weather. The heater has a weird odor when you turn it up high. The bench seats are good, and so are the brakes. The thing you have to watch out for with some of these Fords and Mercurys from the late '60s is the electrical systems can be trouble. Otherwise, you probably could get a year out of it with no major problems."

I said, "The radio is kind of crappy, but it does get the local stations without static or fuzziness. I hope I can get 22-23 miles per gallon driving it. I got enough gas to make it back to Worcester OK, and maybe a few days beyond until my GI Bill check comes. Thanks again, Van. I'll see you at Thanksgiving."

Things were fine with the car until just before Christmas when I had to make a trip up to Vermont for a job interview. The farther north I went, the more miserable the weather became. Not only did I suspect that I blew the interview, but I damn near got into a fight with a guy in downtown Montpelier when my car skidded on some ice at 10 m.ph. into his and caused a very minor dent in his 1959 rusty bucket of bolts. A cop came by and said that it wasn't even $40 worth of damage – there was only a very minor dent in the Comet's right door as well. The guy was loud and may have been drunk, and the cop told him to go home, after he rejected my offer to go through insurance companies. He cursed at me and followed me over 50 miles or so down I-89 before he went off the road and down a hill – it was snowing like hell at that point.

Later, the snow turned to freezing rain and everyone was going 35 mph. I missed a turn and I wound up outside of New London, New Hampshire. As I was pulling into a gas station that was about to close, a cop flashed his lights and wanted to know where the hell I was going driving erratically on a night like this. I told him, the roads were icy, and I slid next to the gas pump unintentionally, but I needed more gas, anyway. The cop and gas station attendant were arguing what was the best way to get back to Worcester. I took the gas station attendant's advice, as the cop angrily gave me a warning. As I drove downhill on a treacherous road, the cop followed me. Then the Comet went into a wicked skid and went off the road at the bottom of the hill, knocking over 2 reflectors and bending a STOP sign. Then came the flashing blue lights from the cop's vehicle. But the cop went into a worse skid than me and ran off the road into some trees about 100 yards back. I saw a sign "To (Rt.) 114," where the gas station attendant told me to go, but I had to go up a hill to get there. I tried to gun it, but only got halfway up the hill and slid back down.

I pleaded with the Comet. "C'mon, you son of a bitch! I don't want to spend a night in jail if that goddamn cop finds me." I tried again, and made it to the top of the hill, but the engine stalled and I cursed again.

I cried, "You piece of shit – you have no power in the snow and ice! How the hell am I supposed to make it through the winter?" I waited two minutes, looked at the dents in my right front fender, started it up again, and I was on my way home. I took a wrong turn, and wound up going way west before I finally made it to my apartment at 1 a.m.

I moved out of my apartment and back into my parents' house in New York the next day. Van came over that weekend. I told him the story of what happened, and he laughed.

"I'm surprised that the dents weren't that bad, and it'd be a waste of money to get them repaired."

"I have to stay the hell out of New Hampshire for a while."

"You need a nickname for this thing. The Falcon was "The Green Toad.""

After bantering a few names around, we came up with "The Vomit Comet," because of the probability of more trouble brewing with the car down the road until I sold it. I got a $35 ticket mailed to me from the New London, NH Police Dept. a month later for reckless driving. I never paid it, or the several parking tickets I owed in Worcester, because I was flat broke.

In February, as I was driving back from a job interview in Rhode Island just past the Lee, Massachusetts exit, I hear a *"bla-bada blabada"* as I accelerated. "Oh, shit – that's got to be a hole in my muffler," I thought. At the time I had a half-ass, low-paying part-time job, which was enough for gas to get me to job interviews and pizza and beer with Van on weekends when I went back home. I called Van, who was my reliable "relief pitcher."

He said, "Meet me over at my parents' house tomorrow night. I hear we've got some relatively warm days upcoming. All my stuff is there because I just worked on my dad's car for him."

At 7 p.m. that night, as I held the flashlight for him, he crawled under the car and yelled, "Holy shit, your manifold is separated from your muffler, and your muffler even has a little rusty hole in it! Your tailpipe is starting to rust, too."

"I can't afford a manifold, a muffler and a tailpipe. I'm fucked!"

"You're not fucked. I can get you a cheap muffler at a junk-yard, and I can attach it to the tailpipe with my soldering gun. There's only a little gap between the manifold and the muffler and I can fuse that together and put a lot of duct tape around it. Park it out in front of the house, and we'll work on it tomorrow night around the same time. I'll drive you to your parents' house."

I called him at 5:30 the next night. Van said, "I got a muffler. C'mon over."

We got under the car and I tried to help him as much as I could. It looked like the duct tape would hold OK. When he got to doing the muffler and tailpipe, the soldering gun started twisting and melting into an "S" shape. We both started laughing.

I said, "I don't believe this piece of shit!"

He replied, "Look at this cheap ass soldering gun! I've never seen anything like that before."

But it worked, even though the muffler was positioned on a little angle. We went over to a college hangout called the Grove, for some pizza and beer. Later, as I pulled out of his parents' driveway to get the wounded Vomit Comet back on the road again, Van yelled to me, "Just don't run over anything and try to avoid any potholes."

I was praying that I could land a good, full-time decent job to move out of my parents' home and get a newer car, but no such luck through March. On April 9th I was coming out of a job interview in Albany and it was snowing like hell – unusual for that time of year there because several days before the temperature had climbed to 70 degrees. They were already plowing the streets. Traffic was creeping along, so I decided to take a detour going downtown when all of a sudden, my driver's side windshield wiper flew off the car into a newly made snowbank. Not exactly the best section of town for this to happen, either. I double-parked the Vomit Comet hoping the car wouldn't get hit or that I wouldn't be mugged and robbed. I proceeded to quickly dig the half-rotted wiper out of the mushy snow. Immediately, I snapped the wiper back onto the car with part of the blade hanging off and the smear was worse than before. There was an open parking space several blocks away close to downtown. After I pulled into it, I rigged the wipers so that I had one good wiper clearing out the middle of the windshield while my head was leaning in a contorted driving position, and the Vomit Comet crawled all the way home at a speed of about 25 mph. Fortunately, I didn't get into an accident, and there were no cops all the way home. Van came to the rescue again that weekend with a pair of wiper blades and inserts. He wanted me to pay him via pizza and beer again. Surprisingly, the Vomit Comet gave me no more problems for the next 4 months.

It was now August, 1974. I quit a part-time job that wasn't very satisfying and much too low-paying. Interviews hit a dead end for me the northeastern U.S. However, I was getting several opportunities for interviews in Wisconsin, so I saved up some money and decided to travel there. Van tuned up the Vomit Comet for me, and he also checked all the hoses, belts and fluids the weekend before I left. Like back in '68, I drove to my uncle's home in Rochester and the car purred like a kitten. Then I took it to Toledo where I slept in a parking lot. From there I drove to Ft. Wayne, Indiana and spent several hours there looking for leads on jobs, but I came up empty.

That night, just outside of Valparaiso, Indiana, the Vomit Comet decided to slow down, As I hit the gas, it started making a whiny, fuzzy sound, losing more and more power until it died, just off a two-lane road. When I tried to start it up, I only heard a "click." I got out of the car, opened up the hood and screamed at it, "You bastard!" I started pacing. How far away was I from the nearest phone booth – about two miles with no sidewalk in the dark? After 10 minutes, wiping away tears and shaking with anger, a nice couple came by and said they'd call the police for me. A cop cruised up to me 20 minutes later.

"Officer, my car died, and I am a long way from home."

"Yeah, I see. You're from New York. Where're you headed?"

"Wisconsin. I'm supposed to be in Madison on Tuesday for a job interview. Can you call AAA for me? I don't know anybody here."

"Ordinarily I wouldn't do that, but we'll get you squared away."

He went back to his vehicle and called AAA. The Vomit Comet was towed to a little "Mom and Pop" gas station in town that the cop said would help me in the morning. After we got there, I thanked him, walked hauling a duffel bag to a cheap motel a few blocks away, checked in, and had a fitful night's sleep.

At 8 o'clock the next morning I walked over to the gas station with my duffel bag in tow. The couple who owned the place were about in their 30s and very nice.

"I know what your problem is, and you ain't gonna like it being a long way from home," the mechanic said.

"Uh oh, can you raise this thing from the dead?"

"Yeah, but it'll take me a few hours. You need a new alternator, solenoid, and battery. I can get the parts as cheap as I can – my wife will call someone to order them – but with labor it might be 3 hours or so until you get out of here and on your way."

"I already checked out of my hotel. Can I stay here and wait in the office?"

"Sure."

I made small talk with them over the next hour or so and somebody brought the parts over. The guy went to work right away and just before noon he said, "You're good to go. I need $180 from you."

I thanked them graciously and I thought, "This puts a humungous dent in my finances."

"Good luck in Wisconsin," his wife said.

"If I make it there."

I had a quick decision to make: Do I take a chance on driving to Wisconsin and hope that I'd get a job right away without being stranded again someplace, or do I should I just head home with my tail between my legs? I chose the latter option. The Comet made it back to Toledo, where I stayed in the same parking lot overnight, with nobody bothering me again. I worked at a job for "cash under the table" at a penny arcade for 10 hours the next day to get a few extra bucks and promptly quit. Then I made a collect call home from a phone booth.

My mother said, "A mental health clinic in Bucyrus, Ohio called. You have an interview there tomorrow if you're still interested."

"Oh, thanks, Mom. I'll call them the first thing in the morning."

I placed a quick call there at 8:30 a.m. and they gave me directions to meet them at a local restaurant at 1 o'clock. But I looked like hell, and I was anxious, and promptly blew the interview. At least they bought me lunch. I had enough time and money to drive to my uncle's house in Rochester, and I was welcomed by him and his family late that night. A free place to stay was a godsend for me.

The Vomit Comet was well-behaved until late October. I was working selling shoes, which I did in college for a year, and also in Albany the summer before I went into the Army – I knew I could make some money doing that. At the end of the month, the tailpipe started falling off and sparks were flying from the car with an ugly dragging sound. I didn't call Van because I was a few blocks away from a Sears automotive shop, so I brought it there. For whatever reason, Sears was the only company that trusted me with a credit card and a $500 limit – I just got the card the week before. When they put it up on a lift, a guy said to a couple of the other mechanics, "You gotta see this!"

A couple of them came over and I could hear them laughing from the door. One guy laughed and said, "Who did this Mickey Mouse job?"

The guy behind the counter asked me, "Did you do that jerry rig yourself?"

"No, but I helped. My buddy broke a soldering gun in the process, and this was the best he could do. But it held up most of the year."

I couldn't fault Van at all, though – he did the best he could with what he had, including the half-ass soldering gun. I wound up getting a new tailpipe and muffler. I couldn't afford to buy another car – I had to keep sinking money into the Vomit Comet, wondering what next was in store for me.

Sure enough, one month later, just before Thanksgiving, the radio died and the internal dash lights became dim: otherwise, the car ran OK. The heater worked when it was up full blast, and it had that weird smell to it. Van and I were out drinking the night before and we both were hung over when he came over to examine it.

"There's no problems with the battery, alternator and solenoid like you had back in Indiana, but I think it must be an electrical problem - maybe some wires and cables are going bad."

"I can't afford to take it to a dealer to get it fixed. I hope I don't have to start taking a freakin' bus to work," I declared.

"Try not to drive it at night and mostly drive it just to and from work," he replied. "You're gonna need another car sooner rather than later."

I did as Van instructed. Fortunately, I got a low–paying job at a hospital not far away. The winter was relatively mild. On very cold nights, I would go out at about 11 o'clock to have a beer at a bar about a mile away to run the engine so it would start OK in the morning, just like I did with the Lambmobile several years earlier. The Vomit Comet surprisingly cooperated all through the winter, putting limited miles on it. Instead of living at home and saving up for another car while I was there, I decided to move out and get my own place for the first time in 15 months.

At the end of April, I finally had enough money to start looking for another car, at last. Besides, a little bit of blue smoke had started coming out of the tailpipe.

"That's a very bad sign," Van said.

"I have to get rid of this thing before it dies and can't be resurrected."

"Are you gonna put an ad in the paper?"

"I think I'm too embarrassed to do that. Maybe I'll ask Danny about where the Lambmobile went a few years ago to be used in a demolition derby. I bet that's where a lot of state cars go to die."

I brought it to a Ford dealer to try to trade it in for a '75 Mercury Bobcat, but there was no way I could afford it. The salesman tried to pitch a '73 Ford Pinto to me, but I didn't trust it after I test drove it. Plus, with 2 or 3 years of payments, I thought it wouldn't be worth it for that used car. Nobody even called me about the Vomit Comet when I finally put an ad in the local paper with a $400 price tag on it, so I went to another Ford dealer looking for a used car. On the lot I noticed a sharp looking purple '71 AMC Javelin.

"Sure – go ahead and test drive it," the salesman said. "You're gonna find that it's a peppy car. Good brakes, too."

I started it up and when I got it out on the road, the car took off like a shot. I thought, "Wow - like it!" But a few miles down the road it shook a little during the U-turn test I always give when I drive a used car. The Javelin bucked a little after I hit the brakes. Otherwise, it rode like a dream and was really comfortable. I wondered if this would be a gas guzzler, too, since prices had doubled in the past year or so. Plus, it had 84,000 miles on it in just 4 years.

When I got back, I asked, "How much do you want for it?"

"$900 including the trade-in for the Comet.

"That's too bad – it's a little bit over my budget, so I have to say no."

"We can work out a financing deal for you."

"Maybe – what else you got in a smaller car?'

I noticed a '71 Dodge Colt on the lot before I drove the Javelin.

Because I thought maybe I could afford a smaller car, I asked, "Can I test drive this one?"

"Take it for a spin."

The Colt was comfortable and rode smoothly, but when I got back from the 3-mile trip, he wanted even more money – $1200 plus the Comet.

"With gas prices up, more people want smaller cars lately," the salesman said.

"I have to pass on this one, and the Javelin for now, but here's my phone number. Call me if you get something else in that I can afford without financing. I want to buy a car outright with a trade for the Comet."

"Ok. We'll let you know."

When I got home, I called Van, told him about the Javelin and asked him if I should've bought it. I told him, "I get paid next week, and I think I can afford it if it's still on the lot."

"Hey, maybe it was a good thing you didn't get the Javelin because it might need new brakes and possibly the power steering is suspect on them. Would've been a hot shit car for a few years, though," he remarked.

I kept wondering about the Javelin, thinking, "Should I buy something that I'd have to sink a couple of hundred bucks into it in the near future, but would be good for the next year or two?"

A week later, during the first week of May, the same car salesman called me.

"The Javelin is still here. We also got a '72 Plymouth Cricket in, if you want to take a look at it."

The Vomit Comet was looking and feeling wretched lately, and I was getting desperate, so I told him, "Yeah. I'll be up there at the end of the day."

I just got paid, and I was hoping to get a better car for my birthday. When I got there, someone was test driving the Javelin, but I test drove the Cricket for 15 minutes out on the local suburban roads at various speeds. I thought, "Nice little car, good trunk room, only 34,000 miles on it, no obvious problems. I have to get something,"

When I got back from the drive, I asked, "How much for it?"

"I'll let it go for $800 including the Comet."

I couldn't pass this up, so I replied, "It's too late to go to the bank. I'll give you $200 in cash to hold it for me, and I'll be back tomorrow morning with the balance, OK?"

"It's a deal," he said, with a smile.

On the one hand, I was thrilled, and on the other hand I wondered what could go wrong with a Plymouth Cricket that was only 3 years old. I couldn't get a hold of Van for his opinion, but I just had to have something else to drive.

On my way to the dealer the next morning, I was about 5 miles away when I was stuck on a two-lane road in back of an old man who was doing 30 in a 45-m.p.h. zone. After a couple of miles of this, I was frustrated, so I decided to pass him at the first opportunity. I pulled out to the left at the first broken line with no cars coming the other way and I slammed my foot down on the accelerator. But half of my foot went right through the rusted floor underneath!

I screamed, "You son of a bitchin' bastard!" I hit the brake with my other foot, and quickly pulled over to the side of the road, yanking my right foot out of the floor.

I yelled to no one, "Two miles away from getting rid of this fucking piece of crap and this happens!"

I got a little calmer as I suddenly remembered I had an old license plate underneath the spare tire in the trunk and I had some duct tape in the glove compartment. I tore a bigger hole next to the accelerator, forced the license plate in between the floor covering and the floor, as some more rust flaked to the ground. Then I was able to tear the duct tape into a few strips on the top of the hole in the floor and I was anxiously on my way to trade in the Vomit Comet. I made it to the dealer's without the damn thing falling apart completely.

A few minutes later I sped off with the Plymouth Cricket, sighing in relief. No more Vomit Comet! Hallelujah! They probably chopped up that junker for parts.

CHAPTER 4

The Chirping Cricket: 1975

When I drove the Cricket home, it felt like a cloud compared to the Comet. This was the first car I ever had with bucket seats, which was cool. Nothing was wrong with the interior, and all the buttons and knobs worked fine. The maximum reading on the speedometer was 90, but I didn't foresee when I would ever have to go that fast. I wondered why I never heard of a Plymouth Cricket before, but I didn't care because I surely was convinced that this would be another short-term car for me. When I got a better, higher paying job, hopefully within the next year or sooner, I'd splurge for a brand-new car.

That weekend I called Van to come over and see the Cricket. We zoomed around the area after I bought my first tank of gas.

"This probably gets great mileage per gallon," I said.

"It's a small enough 4-cylinder engine," he replied.

I drove down the road for several miles and I said, "I think I got a great deal for something with only a little over 34,000 miles on it."

He said, "I just noticed something – your odometer hasn't moved at all. The thing must be broken. You don't know what the hell the exact mileage is. No wonder they sold it to you like this. I hope you didn't buy something with 134,280 miles on it."

"Damn! No – this thing can't have 134,280 miles on it. It's only 3 years old. Let's bring it home and take a look under the hood again."

He took a look at it and said, 'I don't know. I think there's a cable in there that's somehow connected to the transmission or to gears in the speedometer and you might have to take apart your whole dashboard, or other things I've never messed with. But it doesn't look like there are any broken cables. Maybe a Plymouth dealer can help you, but it'll cost you your ass, I bet."

"No way can I afford that. What's the danger in not getting it fixed?"

"Well, when you go to trade it in, nobody will know how many miles you actually have on it. That could be good or bad. When you trade it in, if they notice it, tell 'em that you first noticed the problem in May of '75 and you didn't know what to do about it."

"I have to start putting away money for a new vehicle now, then. I'm gonna let it go within the next year, hopefully."

"I don't see anything else wrong with the car at all, though. Let's find out whatever we can about a Plymouth Cricket. There's no manual in the glove compartment."

"That's another thing I forgot all about because I was in such a hurry to get rid of the Vomit Comet and get out of the dealer's. I wanted to buy almost any car better."

"I'll be surprised if you have any problems with it in the near future, though. But you never know."

"I think 'You never know' is the biggest lesson I've learned in life so far."

"You used to say that most of life is based on luck, and you can rarely be sure of anything in the future."

"I don't totally believe that any more, but for me that seems to be the way it is for cars, jobs, apartments, and women. Anyway, as long as it's running great, I want to start taking some trips this summer when I can."

I was working at a psychiatric unit of a general hospital. One of the patients was a sociopath/druggie who bullshitted his way into the unit for several days because he allegedly made a suicidal gesture in order to postpone going to jail. He was also a long-time car mechanic at one of the local garages. After group therapy one afternoon, he said to me with a smile, "I saw you pull up in a Plymouth Cricket in the parking lot this morning."

"Yeah, I just bought it second-hand. Do you know much about the '72 Plymouth Cricket? The odometer on this thing is broken."

He chuckled, "All I'll tell you is be careful driving it over 60 (m.p.h.) and treat it like a baby, and maybe you'll get 2 years out of it. A guy pushed in a '71 Cricket to our garage and the engine was blown – he wound up abandoning it. The Cricket is a makeover of a cheap-ass English or European car that Chrysler converted several years ago. They made it for '71, '72, and '73 before they scrapped it. I heard that most of them had engine, cooling system or suspension problems."

"So far, it runs great, and everything else is working fine. The interior is good, too. But from what you say, sounds like I bought a crapmobile."

"Good luck, and don't bother bringing it in anyplace to fix the odometer," he laughed.

I followed his advice. At the end of the month, I drove it up to Burlington, VT to hang out at Lake Champlain and then to Montreal to see a baseball game, as most of the cars zoomed by me.

I didn't mind driving like an old man. There were no problems with the Cricket, and it ran fine for the whole month of June. "Maybe I did get a great deal on this little car," I thought.

The 4th of July weekend ended the honeymoon. I had a few days off, so I decided to take a trip to Lake Winnipesaukee in New Hampshire. I packed up the car early in the morning of July 3rd and I got only a mile away when I noticed smoke coming out from underneath the hood. Quickly, I turned around and by the time the Cricket staggered home the engine was smoking up badly as I pulled into the driveway. I hurried inside and called Van, who happened to be off work for most of the weekend.

"Van, I really need your help. The engine's smoking up so bad the hood is too hot to open. I hope I don't need a new radiator or something. Any chance you can make it over here?"

"Give me about an hour or so and I'll be over."

Van got there about an hour and a half later and I opened the hood latch. He propped up the hood, looked around and said, "Where the hell is your fan?"

We looked more carefully, and he suddenly said, laughing, "Look! This goddamn thing had a plastic fan!"

The fan had shattered and had only one half of one of the melted blades were left on it – the other half fell right off underneath the car. When we took out what was left of the fan, I didn't know whether to laugh or cry.

"I have never, ever seen anything like this before," Van giggled as he shook his head.

"It's a damn good thing it happened here instead of some rural road in Vermont or New Hampshire, where I don't know anyone. I don't know how I would've coped with that."

"Well, let's go to some junkyards to see if we can get a real metal fan to put on this thing."

I was still stunned, as the Harold Melvin and the Blue Notes' song "Bad Luck" was playing on the radio in his car. That was an omen for the day, as we went to a few junkyards in the area and no luck. It wasn't until Saturday, on the 5th, that we discovered a junkyard that had a metal fan from a '71 Cricket, and I promptly bought it. Van put it on for me and it fit fine.

As we went out for my usual treat of pizza and beer later, he said, "Maybe that was a sign from above for you not to go up to New Hampshire."

"Yeah, at least when it comes to cars. The Lambmobile actually kind of died there when Danny drove it into a river up there one night several years ago. I'm calling this car the Chirping Cricket."

"Well, the rest of the car is OK. None of the wires melted or burned and the battery and exhaust system are OK underneath. You ought to get a new radiator, though."

"I can't afford a new radiator right now."

"Then you better fill it up with water and anti-freeze and buy a can of Stop Leak, just in case something happens."

"OK – let's go do it. It's the middle of the summer, so I probably won't need anti-freeze until sometime in October. My parents have some anti-freeze in their garage if I need it."

We filled up the radiator with water and put in some Stop-Leak as a precautionary measure, and that really seemed to help. The fan and the radiator were back to normal – not a drip or drop anywhere. For the next month, the car ran great, and I even drove it out to Pittsburgh and eastern Ohio for futile job interviews in August.

I saw Don in Pittsburgh for the first time in a few years. He laughed when I told him the story about the Vomit Comet, and as for the Cricket, he never heard of any car having a plastic fan. As we took a ride, he also said, "I've never seen a Plymouth Cricket, but it runs well. It's comfortable. I like the bucket seats. The radio seems to be OK."

The Chirping Cricket was well-behaved well into the fall, even when I took a trip to Toronto to see some long-lost relatives. I had no idea how many miles I put on the car, but it was getting very good gas mileage. The suspension system appeared to have no defects, and the tires were wearing well.

One morning in early November (as the weather got colder) the lights on the Cricket got a little dimmer, the horn wasn't as loud, and the car took a little longer to start. I didn't have to go to work until 3 p.m., so I drove it over to a Sears automotive so I could use my Sears credit card.

The guy behind the counter asked me, "Hey, you want a Die-Hard for your car, don't you?"

"No. I plan on getting rid of this car by no later than next spring. I just need the cheapest thing you got."

They sold me a cheap small Sears battery with a year guarantee and installed it. "It's a lot like the same one you had in there," he said. The new battery cured the current ills of the Cricket - they told me the electrical system was OK – not like the Vomit Comet. I could breathe easier for a while, hoping it would last through the winter, at least.

But misfortune struck again. A week later the car was starting to leak water again, so I called Van.

"You really ought to splurge for a new radiator, if you think it's worth it," he said.

"I'd rather just buy a cheap new car and have a 5-year loan. I've been saving money for one lately. I just can't afford to even look for something until after Thanksgiving," I said.

"All right. Bring it over to my house tomorrow night and let's drain the radiator, put in a mixture of water and anti-freeze and a can of Stop Leak again."

"Can I bring it over right after you get home from work? I'm doing a month on the night shift, so I'll be just getting up from sleeping."

"Yeah, but we can't go out for pizza and beer. I have to be here for Rosie." Van's wife, Rosie was due with their first child any day now.

"I can't do any drinking, anyway. But I could get a pizza to go from some place over there, later on, if you want."

"No, that's OK. Just c'mon over tomorrow around 5 o'clock. It doesn't take that long to get it done."

The next evening, just as it was starting to get dark, I helped him, and the job was done in an hour. I told him I'd buy him a Christmas present next month. The Cricket chirped along again.

Two weeks later I started filling up the Cricket with water and/or leftover anti-freeze about every 3 or 4 days because it was leaking again. Fortunately, I just landed a new job in New Hampshire with a $5000 raise to start on December 8th. Much of my spare time was spent test driving new cars at several local dealers – this time I swore I wouldn't settle for a used clunker. I was worried that if I came up empty, the Cricket might get its last chirps in before dying at the outset of winter, and I had just enough money to buy a brand-new car with a 3-year loan. I tried to get a Dodge Colt or an AMC Pacer, but those dealers wouldn't give me more than $400 to $500 on a trade-in for the Cricket, even though I washed, waxed, and detailed it as best I could.

Less than a week before I was to move away, I test drove a '76 Pontiac Astre. "I like this car, and I like the design," I thought, as I drove it through the suburban roads of Albany and Schenectady. "Power steering, power brakes, bucket seats, good trunk space, and it looks like a little sedan."

The salesman asked, "How do you like it?"

"I like it, but what can you give me on a trade for my car?"

"I'm gonna have somebody look it over for a few minutes."

"If I were to buy the Astre, I'd want that yellow one in the showroom," I said.

The guy who drove it was back in less than 5 minutes, and he and the salesman went in to talk to their manager. A few minutes later the salesman came out and said, "We'll give you $850. Does that sound fair to you?"

"It's a deal," I responded.

I couldn't pass it up. I tried to stay as cool and disguise my giddiness as much as I could while I signed all the papers. My mother, who was a bank officer, helped me get a 3-year loan through her bank (better than the dealer's rate), but she had to co-sign it for me because of my meager credit history.

The Cricket had its last chirp on December 4th, and I drove away with my first new car – with only 7 miles on it! What a feeling to roll down the highway in a sharp looking little vehicle with that new car smell to it!

CHAPTER 5

The Flameout Astre: 1975-1978

Proudly driving the sporty Astre into New Hampshire felt like a big deal for me, and I had no suspicions that anything could possibly go wrong with a brand-new car. I never had such a pleasant, relaxing feeling before. The weather wasn't as cold up there as I expected at first, but soon it started snowing a couple of times a week, creating a kind of natural blanket over the hood of the car. Fortunately, my new job was only several blocks away from where I was living. So, as long as the morning temperature was at least 15 degrees above zero, I could walk to work. Once January came, that was a different story, however. Every night when the temperature got down to single digits or below zero, the car wouldn't start in the morning. If I left it in a place where the sun would hit the hood, it would start up when I came home for lunch. I took it to a local Pontiac dealer.

"OK, we'll take a look at it," said the dealer.

A half hour later, the guy at the desk said, "There's nothing wrong with it."

I was surprised, but at least there was no charge because it was under warranty. But it still wouldn't start for most mornings in the next two weeks, and I took it back to the same dealer.

I sternly asked the man behind the desk, "This is a new car with less than 1000 miles on it. Why won't it kick over in the morning? Hell, it's not THAT cold out."

I overheard a mechanic who was hanging around saying, "This guy's a pain in the ass."

I started bitching to them. "Hey, this is a brand-new car under warranty and a dealer has to fix the problem. I don't want to get the Better Business Bureau involved here."

The mechanic turned around, came in the doorway and sarcastically said, "Look, pal, they made this vehicle with an aluminum block engine. I don't know how long you've lived here with your New York plates, but it gets a hell of a lot colder up here than there most nights, and the engine has to have the oil warm for the car to start."

"How the hell am I supposed to cure that problem? Do I have to wake up at 2:30 a.m. and go out and drive it around for 5 miles every night?"

"You need to get an engine block heater. We don't sell them here, but auto parts stores do."

I went to an auto parts store and bought an electric dipstick for about $25, but I had to buy two extension cords to hook it up to the house and hope nobody would steal the dipstick or the cords from the driveway off the street. I did this every night the temperature would get into the low teens, and this worked well for about a month. Then one morning, it got to 33 below zero and the car wouldn't even start until later in the afternoon, even with the contraption hooked up to the oil. I called Van that Saturday morning before he went to his part-time job at the gas station.

"Hey, Van, this new car I got is appropriate for its color – it's a lemon."

I went on to explain the problem I was having, bitching about the rude treatment from the mechanic at the dealer, and my cumbersome attempt at resolving the situation.

Van said, "The mechanic at the dealer's sounds like a prick, from what you say. But that still doesn't sound good for a new car. I'll call around to some people I know and ask if they know anyone who owns a Pontiac Astre. I'll get back to you later on."

About an hour later he called me back saying, "Maybe you did get a lemon. A couple of people have told me that it turns out that the Pontiac Astre is the same thing as a Chevy Vega, only they dressed up the body and interior to look better and they've tried to correct the burning oil problem most Vegas have."

"So, this is like putting a Brook Brothers suit on a wretch."

"If you think the temperature is gonna get below the teens, you could go out and have a beer at some bar close to 11 before you go to bed, and then go home and put the electric dipstick in. Otherwise, you might be screwed again."

"I should have done some research before I bought this one."

"By the way, register your car up there in New Hampshire. You need to do that anyway, and there won't be any smart-ass remarks like that mechanic at the dealer said to you."

"Yeah, I was gonna do that this week one day on my lunch hour. I heard there is another Pontiac dealer at the next town about 20 miles away, and I'll go there if I have to. Thanks, Van."

I drove the Astre a lot for the first year. My father was dying of cancer, so I was making trips home almost every weekend. I had a mishap where I stopped suddenly for a red light one night in late February and skidded a little bit, but the guy behind me also skidded on the icy patch and hit my rear bumper.

There were two teenagers who got out of the car behind me.

"Oh, no – my dad's not gonna be happy," the kid who was the driver said, sadly.

"Here's a quarter," I said to his friend. Go call the cops at that phone booth near the McDonald's over there. We'll wait here until a cop comes."

"It doesn't look like my car was damaged at all, but your bumper is hanging just a tiny bit loose," the kid observed. We exchanged writing down licenses, registrations and insurance information.

The cop who investigated said the damage was minor enough that he wasn't going to report it.

My bumper would cost $65 to fix, but there was no dent in it – since it was only hanging slightly loose, I easily lifted it back into shape. The kid's father called me the next day, and he was very nice about everything. My insurance and the kid's insurance wouldn't pay for the mishap because of the deductibles. I told his father that I felt sorry for him because he was only 19 and I think the ice was "an act of God" causing the accident, and we agreed that he didn't have to worry because there was no damage to his car. As time went on, anytime I went over a bump or hit a pothole, it would sag a little and after I parked, I'd lift the bumper back into place.

Just before the 6-month warranty expired, the starter conked out at a mall about 20 miles away from home. I thought, angrily, "Dammit, this is supposed to be a new car – the starter shouldn't die this soon!" Luckily, I had a AAA membership, and I was not far from a Pontiac dealer, so I had it towed there.

When I talked to the mechanic there about the problems I was having and asked, "Why the hell are these things happening with a car not quite 6 months old?"

"Sorry about the starter. That's just bad luck, I guess. We'll put in a new one for you ASAP."

"What about the aluminum block engine in the freezing weather? Would I be better off living in someplace like Florida driving an Astre?"

He laughed and said, "If you lived there, I bet the Astre would eventually overheat a lot and the engine might eventually get warped. This car will probably last a lot longer if you were a 'snowbird' (living 7 to 8 months up north and in Florida through the winter). It's a great car for Hawaii or San Francisco."

"I wish I'd known this when I bought the car."

Right then, I knew I had to get rid of this freakin' lemon around the time the 60,000-mile warranty would expire.

Fortunately, it was a relatively cool summer in 1976. I drove it out to the Midwest to look up some "long-lost" relatives and the warmest day was 82 degrees. There was no chance of the Astre overheating. Over the next several months the odometer escalated. When I drove it home for weekends, I changed the oil myself a couple of times and Van gave it a tune-up once. One Sunday in the fall, it overheated once when I was stuck in traffic coming home from a New England Patriots game in Foxboro, Massachusetts. The Astre made it through the wicked cold and snowy winter with no significant problems, and the electric dipstick worked like a magic wand. However, one very snowy night in March 1977, the Astre skidded off the road and got stuck in a snowbank. I walked about a half mile to a new house where I was living – I knew my housemate, Jack, would help me get it out the next morning. The next day we noticed that overnight it was mashed in with snow and ice by a snowplow. It took hours for us to get it out of there and, although there were no dents in it, the engine ran rougher than it should have in cold weather. It seemed like I was driving a vehicle several years older than it actually was. I put 30,000 miles on it for the first 15 months I had the car.

Except for having to get four new tires right after Memorial Day, the Astre was very well behaved. But that summer on the open road it started feeling like it had double the miles on it, and it didn't quite have the power it had when it was new. I got a major warning signal about Pontiacs in June. My friend Dolph started bitching about his '73 Pontiac Ventura that recently died.

"I'm pissed," he angrily said. "No car bought new should ever bite the dust at 61,500 miles. Right after the engine warranty expired, too. I'll never buy another Pontiac again."

"The Pontiac dealer's service department in this town isn't worth a crap, either," I said.

He remarked, "I need something ASAP. We have another kid on the way next month. I may get a '77 Dodge Aspen I just test drove last night."

"Good luck, "I replied.

I thought, after this interaction, that as soon as my loan was paid off, if not even sooner, I would never buy another Pontiac again, too.

Two months later, as I was driving back to New England from New York, the Astre's engine was sounding a little louder than usual. It gradually started to lose some power as I was getting through Vermont. I tried shifting from Drive to Low gear and back to Drive, but it wouldn't go back into Drive.

I shouted, "Oh, you bastard! Don't die on me before I make it home!" The Astre slowly flamed out and limped home like a 90-year-old man. I had to drive with the emergency flashers on for about 75 miles, making the usual 3-hour trip in 4 ½ hours. I had no choice but to take it to the local Pontiac dealer early the next morning.

"Groucho" behind the counter remembered me and asked with a snarl, "What's wrong with your car now?"

"I can't get the car out of low gear. It started gradually losing power about 80 miles away from here yesterday."

"We'll take a look at it. You gonna wait?"

"Yeah. I'm stuck here."

An hour later, a mechanic, a nicer guy than last year, came in and said, "Your transmission cable is broken."

Groucho added, "Since it's over 36,000 miles, it's no longer covered by the warranty."

"How much will it cost?"

"A little over $200."

An hour and a half later the job was done, costing $205. I thought, "There goes another hunk of cash sunk into this chintzy machine. At least they took my American Express card because I don't have enough money in my checking account, just getting back from a vacation. Dolph was right about Pontiacs – this shouldn't happen to a car only 20 months old. Good thing I get paid in a few days – my rent and utilities are due at the end of the month, so I'll have to lay low through Labor Day weekend."

Right after Labor Day, at the end of this blazing hot summer, the engine overheated again. This time, as I was taught by Van with another of my previous "crapmobiles," I did the anti-freeze/water mix myself. I still prayed for a cool fall and a mild winter because I didn't trust the Astre to make it through another harsh winter.

After the first cold night in November, the original Delco battery died. Luckily, it happened at my mother's house when I was home for the weekend. I called Van again.

Hey, Van. Do believe the original Delco battery in this piece of junk died? I only got 2 years out of it!"

"You got jumper cables?"

"No, I just called AAA."

"Smart move, as long as you got AAA."

"What do you suggest for a new one? Sears?"

"Yeah. You could go over there and get a Die-Hard. C'mon over here afterwards and we'll have a couple of beers. Rosie is at her parents' house with the baby all day."

"OK, I don't know how much time and money it'll take, but I'll see you early in the afternoon, probably."

AAA came and got the Astre started for me. I promptly went over to Sears to get one of their Die-Hard batteries installed to assure myself that this wouldn't happen again during the upcoming frigid winter. Just before Christmas the electric dipstick went kaput, so I called in sick and walked 2 miles to an auto parts store in the bone chilling cold to buy a new one. Other than those mishaps, the Astre made it through another frigid and snowy winter without any serious problems.

At the beginning of March, my no longer new automobile hit the 55,000-mile mark and I really started to pay the price for all the miles I put on it in the past two and a quarter years. I noticed it started running rough around town and only a little smoother on the interstates. Then, at the end of April, as I drove to work, I thought I saw a faint puff of blue smoke coming out of the exhaust. On my lunch break I asked Dolph to hit the accelerator quick while it was in Park (gear) so I could take a look.

He asked, "See anything?"

I replied, "Yeah. My suspicions are confirmed. Bad news. Thanks, Dolph."

I said to myself, "That's it – the Astre is flaming out already, just like Chevy Vegas do. I got to get rid of this dressed up junker ASAP." I knew this day might come sometime during the year, but despite taking a vacation to Florida earlier in April, I had stayed in every weekend all winter and saved up some money to put a down payment on a more reliable vehicle. On May 1st, I went out looking for a new car.

I test drove cars at 5 different dealers. First, I drove a Dodge Omni at one dealership. Then I drove a Dodge Colt at another place, which I liked better, having rented one recently in Florida. The Volkswagen Golf was nice, too – I couldn't afford their convertible, though. The Buick Skylark seemed good, but the salesman was so high pressured toward me, he pissed me off – he virtually tried to bully me into buying the car. When he gave me his card, I ripped it up. I didn't really like the Ford Fairmont as much, but I thought maybe I'd consider buying it if I came up empty. Every one of the salesmen all seemed to say the same thing: "You have high mileage on your car for a '76 and you never had the rear bumper fixed. Those things knock down the trade-in value." They also knew the reputation of the car – the Astre was discontinued after 1977. Every one of the bastards insulted me with the trade-in offers – no more than $1600 toward any car I wanted! The sticker price on the Astre when it was new was $3900 and that was only 2 ½ years ago. I was pissed, but I felt I couldn't afford to look for another car much longer.

I asked Dolph about his Dodge Aspen. "So far, it's OK. I haven't really had any trouble with it yet, and I've had it for about 9 or 10 months."

I said to him, "Marilyn (a social worker who worked with Dolph and me) told me she has a cousin who's a salesman at the Plymouth dealer's right outside of town. I see ads for the Plymouth Volare on TV, and I hear it's the same car essentially as the Aspen."

"Check it out. You got nothing to lose by test driving it."

"Yeah. I'm desperate. I have to get rid of this 'Flameout Astre.'"

Marilyn's cousin was a nice guy, but he said the same thing the other dealers said about the high mileage and the bumper. I test drove the Volare and it had a bench seat instead of the Astre's bucket seats, and it was a 6-cylinder instead of a 4-cylinder, but it rode smoothly and was comfortable. After going back and forth with him for a couple of days, he agreed to take $1800 on a trade-in for the Astre. I noticed that the Volare I test drove had a very small lump on the moulding in the rear bumper.

I asked, "You'll get that smoothed out or replaced, won't you?"

"As is – that's part of the deal."

"C'mon – what if I buy one of the others on the lot?"

"The price goes down on the trade-in, and every other one we have in stock right now costs more. This one's only got less than 100 miles on it. Do you want it, or not?"

I thought, "So much for being a nice guy. I need a new car now, and this guy's got me by the balls. I hope I can get 3 years out of it with no problems."

I took the deal, after going back and forth with him for two days, arguing over the ridiculous cost of "dealer prep." I had about 6 months to pay off the loan on the Astre and I had to get a 3-year loan on this one.

"You have the title?"

"No. I must be home. I don't carry it around with me in the glove compartment."

"You can't trade in your car without us getting the title."

"I'll come back tomorrow afternoon with it."

But the title wasn't at my place. I started panicking. I called my mother, who was part of negotiating the loan at the bank where she worked when I bought the Astre in New York.

She said, "Hang on. It might be here."

As it turned out, my mother had it and she said she'd send it to me right away. I called the salesman and told him what happened. He said he'd try to hold it for 3 days max. It took me 3 days before I brought the Astre and the title up to him. When I got there, the salesman said his boss agreed to fix the moulding, but it wouldn't be ready for me to pick it up for a couple more days.

The Astre seemed to want to flame out with me until the end. When I went back to finally close the deal, I thought, "Just take this god-damn junker away from me before it falls apart or dies. I want to drive away with the Volare now."

I don't recall ever seeing anyone drive another Pontiac Astre any-where, after that day.

CHAPTER 6

The Rusty Volare: 1978-1985

I was still bothered by the lousy trade-in money I was offered for the Astre. In fact, I kept thinking about the '78 Dodge Colt I drove for a week on a trip to Florida the month before. "Maybe I could get a Dodge Colt with the next car I'd buy in a few years," I thought.

The Volare was a light blue 2-door coupe with cloth bench seats and a 225 slant 6 engine, and because it was a 6-cylinder car, gas mileage was only average. The car ran great during the first few months I had it. I even drove it up to the top of Mt. Washington in New Hampshire in July with no problems. Every passenger I had, front and back seat, did not complain about the comfort and the ride (the Astre had more road noise). But later that summer I noticed that the radio wasn't as good as some of the other cars I had. So, right after Labor Day, I had a cassette player put in. I liked playing my cassettes better, anyway. For the next few years, I seldom used the radio except for some sports game. The Volare made it through the first winter in good shape. In fact, I had no problems at all with the car for about the first year. I thought, "I'm not used to this. I finally got a reliable car, after all these years."

The Volare hit the 18,000-mile mark in April,1979, and the tires were wearing unevenly, so I had a front-end alignment done at a local garage. I figured that February through April there were potholes and frost heaves around on the northern New England roads, and maybe that's why I needed one. I should have been more attentive to the tires because the mechanic showed me that the treads were worn so unevenly that I should purchase four new ones. I seized the moment when I noticed that there was a sale on Goodyear tires locally, and I bought them, figuring the four new tires were good for another 40,000 miles, at least. Van told me once that there were times when in order to cut corners on costs, dealers would put mediocre tires on new cars as part of the so-called "dealer prep" fee most of them charged. I surmised, "What the hell – I won't have that problem again for quite a while."

A big warning signal popped up not long afterwards. One morning going into work I smiled and greeted Dolph in the parking lot with the typical smart-ass joking line, "Hey, Dolph – how's your *ASSSSS*…pen?"

He replied, "I'm sorry I bought this car. I'm starting to have various problems pop up with it – transmission, suspension, rough idling, especially at the end of the winter."

"Uh oh. I hope this isn't an omen for me. I have just about the same car, but one year younger. I hope they corrected a lot of potential problems with the '78 models."

The omen came to pass two weeks later when the transmission gears were either slightly off or occasionally started missing altogether over a period of a few days. I was warned that the local Chrysler-Dodge-Plymouth dealer where I bought the car had a poor reputation for service, so I took it to another place recommended by my landlord. Unlike the Astre, the cable wasn't broken, but the warranty covered only 12,000 miles for transmission problems. It turned out the car had slowly leaking transmission fluid and it cost over $200 dollars to fix the problem.

I was pissed. When I paid the bill, I told the guy behind the counter, "That shouldn't happen to a fairly new car, dammit!"

"Hey, good thing you brought it in rather than waiting 2 weeks or so. You coulda been looking at major engine problems," the mechanic said.

Fortunately, I never had that problem again, but there were more "dammits" ahead. The summers of 1978 and 1979 were hot ones, and there was no air conditioning in the car. I didn't think I needed it because I was living in New Hampshire, and it would've been another expensive option. Because of this, by August, the upholstery showed signs of wear, with tiny rips and a sweat stain on the driver's side.

That September, I moved to Florida (back in school again) and the Volare had almost 30,000 miles on it. I had to get two new front tires and a front-end alignment just before I left because of uneven tread wear again. I also had problems with the brake pads wearing down fast, and I had to get new ones for the front. I hoped that maybe the warmer Florida weather would mean less problems mechanically with the Volare, and maybe if I hung in there with it for 2 years, there wouldn't be many expenses or defects surfacing. My plan was to sell it around Christmas, 1981. At that time, I might be able to get a good deal on a 1981 model car some dealer would try to dump for the new year's inventory. The worst-case scenario would be that I would keep sinking money into it and run it into the ground. But I figured that would be unlikely.

Man, was I wrong! When I arrived in Florida, a lot of the chrome was covered with pesky "love bugs." I was so busy looking for a place to live and registering for school that after about 5 days later, I noticed little rusty dots all over the grille. I found out that the damn bugs were acidic – they only appear in Florida about once or twice a year, and it was my luck that I literally ran into hundreds of the little bastards in one of their peak seasons. I promptly washed my car. I thought I wouldn't have any more problems with rust in the warm weather and no salt on the roads during the winter to eat up any ice. Fortunately, I rented an apartment less than 100 yards away from the ocean, and even though my outside parking space was unprotected from the elements, I didn't give any problems related to parking a car there a second thought. One windy weekend at the end of September I stayed home, except for walking on the beach and not using the car at all. That Sunday afternoon I decided that the salty film on the Volare needed to come off ASAP. I hadn't washed the car in over two weeks, since the love bugs were gone. To my shock, after I was done there was more rust on various parts of the car. I brought it in to the local Plymouth dealer to get an oil change because they were having a special deal on a few certain maintenance procedures.

"Hey, my car is only about 16 months old and it's starting to show rust already," I complained.

The guy at the service desk told me, "I see you're living right on the ocean. You have to rinse off the car every 5 to 7 days, or you'll just keep getting more rust on it."

A mechanic hanging around chimed in, "Especially with a Volare or Aspen because we start to see rust and body integrity problems with them after a year or two."

The service desk guy added, "Rust isn't covered by any warranty you have, either."

From that point on, I either washed or thoroughly rinsed off the slowly rusting Volare every week. The paint was starting to slightly fade from being in the Florida sun all the time, on top of the last few sunny, hot summers in New England. "What a shitbox for a new car from a reputable organization like Chrysler," I thought.

But at least the windows didn't shatter from the Florida heat and humidity. I saw a black Cadillac get one of its dark tinted windows blown out in an outdoor mall parking lot one 90-degree humid day, as I was coming out of a store. From that point on, I left each of the four of the windows in the Volare a crack open wherever I parked it. But that soon created another problem – parts of the chrome on the dashboard, directional arm, and gear shift quickly got little rust spots on them when I parked outside of my residence.

I flew back home for the Christmas holidays and let my landlord use the car for three weeks. When I got back, I had to carefully clean out a couple of his kids' sticky lollipops from the upholstery in the front and back seats that resulted in more little rips. I was upset initially, but I couldn't complain vociferously because he had charged me such low rent for the apartment (overlooking the ocean) that I "bit my tongue." I rationalized, "Kids will be kids," and there would have been nobody else at that time to whom I could entrust the rusty Volare. A couple of weeks later I was drinking a couple of beers with him while we were watching an NFL playoff game. Suddenly he told me something that was a shock.

He looked at me with a half-smile while a commercial was on, and said, "I've been on the run from the law in Ohio for the past 6 years!"

I shockingly tuned to him and said, "Wow! What the hell did you do?"

"I drove a getaway car for an armed robbery 6 years ago. I didn't get caught and high tailed it down here."

"Don't tell me anything more. I didn't hear you say that."

I didn't lend him the Volare again. His own car (actually his wife's) was a '79 Chevy Chevette that was totaled from an accident in early December, and in his spare time he and one of his friends were trying to get it to run so he could get it back on the road eventually, even with the bent frame. In the meantime, he somehow got an under-the-table cash deal for a '70 AMC Gremlin hatchback rattle trap that helped him get around town to go to the store and for other various business and family errands. I didn't ask about how he got the plates, or if he had a driver's license, or was living under an assumed name. The less I knew, the better.

Six weeks into 1980 things started taking a turn for the worse with the rust prone Volare. I was slowly pulling into a red light on U.S. 1, and I noticed a Dodge RAM Charger truck behind me that wasn't stopping. I had no time to get out of the way; in my rear-view mirror he seemed to be coming at me around 40 m.p.h. I quickly braced myself as much as I could, putting my left arm in front of my face, and tugging at the seat belt with my right arm (to avoid going through the windshield) and "BAM!" The bastard didn't even put on his brakes! My car got the worst of it by far, with the rear end smashed in. I felt like I was a quarterback blindsided by a defensive end. I just sat in the car for a minute, stunned, or in shock. As soon as I got out, I said to the guy, "What the hell?" Then, I added, "Where are your brains? You didn't even stop!"

He mumbled something semi-coherently about not noticing the light changed to red, and he asked, "You OK, man? I'm OK." At that moment, a policeman pulled up. Some dude came running across the street also trying to intervene for the guy in the truck – apparently, he was a friend of his.

"My man here ain't high, he ain't drunk," he pleaded with the cop.

"I'm all right. I don't think I got hurt," I said to the cop.

An elderly couple, who was in their car a short distance behind the truck in the next lane, stopped and got out of their vehicle and said to all of us that they saw the accident. It turned out that there was no substance abuse involved on the part of the guy driving the truck, but he was supposed to have corrective lenses, and he wasn't wearing them. The cop investigating the accident gave me the phone number of a reputable nearby auto body shop where I could have the car towed. As I was about to cross the street to a phone booth to call the place, the guy's "friend" came up to me saying, "Hey, sucker – why'd you do my man like that?'

The elderly lady said, "Don't answer him."

Her husband said, "Be careful."

I calmly gestured to the dude saying, "Don't call me sucker. You be cool with me; I'll be cool with you. The cop is still in his car there."

He asked, in a more subdued voice, "What happened? Did you tell the cop my man was fucked up?"

I calmly explained, "Your man didn't have his glasses on. He couldn't tell how far he was between me and him and he couldn't stop in time."

The truck, probably because it was so big, didn't have much damage and it was still drivable. The dude went over to the cop in his car and said he would drive the guy home who hit me. I heard the cop say, "Good, get out of here." They left and the cop took a statement from the couple who left. I called the autobody shop, who took AAA, and they soon arrived and towed the Volare there.

"I'd say offhand there's a 50-50 chance your car is totaled," the auto body guy said. I called my landlord, who gave me a ride home, and then called my insurance company to inform them of the ugly details of the accident. The driver of the truck had no insurance, but at least I was covered through Nationwide for accidents involving uninsured drivers.

The next morning, I had a wicked whiplash effect in my neck, along with some other minor aches and pains. I got a ride to school with my landlord, but he couldn't drive me home. Fortunately, a girl in my class who saw the aftermath of the accident drove me back to my apartment later and, as a stroke of luck, she became a real good girlfriend for the next few months. At least something good came from out of the debacle. My insurance man called me two days later.

He said, "Your Volare was about $50 away from being totaled, but the body shop is going to fix it up. It may take at least a month, though."

"Joe, can you get me a rental? I got to have some wheels, man."

"I checked into that for you. We got a place down there that will give you a Chevy Nova, but it won't be a new car. It's 4 or 5 miles away from where you live, but right near that auto body shop."

"When can I pick it up?"

"Somebody who's using it is gonna bring it back to them tomorrow. It might take a couple of days. Here's the number to call them."

I scribbled down the phone number he gave and thanked him. It wasn't until a few days later that I got a white '74 Chevy Nova coupe hatchback, paid for by my insurance company. I had no problems with the Nova other than the fact that it rode stiffly, and the radio was just fair. It took about 6 weeks to get what I now called the "Rusty Volare" back on the road. The car felt like it was five years old instead of two. On March 31st, I had to leave Florida for several months because I ran out of money and wound up getting a job back in New England. Nobody was hiring in Florida unless I would consent to sell shoes again, like I did years before.

A month later, I stopped into a store in southern Vermont for a few minutes and when I came out, there was an ugly gash in my left rear panel about 4 inches under the gas cap. A few people were slowly walking and talking outside the store.

I asked, "Hey, did any of you see who did this?"

An elderly lady said, "There was a truck with out of state plates that had some pipes hanging out of the rear of it, but the guy came and went quickly. I didn't hear anything scraping though."

At that point I wondered if it was worth it to contact the insurance company again, or just say, "The hell with it," and run the Rusty Volare into the ground. I chose the latter option. I had no money to buy a new car, or even a decent used car. I couldn't afford my insurance cost to go up any more. The Rusty Volare was crappy, but I thought maybe in 2 or 3 years I could get something new once the burden of school expenses had subsided.

I drove back and forth between New England and Florida two more times that year, and I went through another set of tires as well as needing front end alignments because of the lousy suspension system. Like the Eddie Rabbit song out that year, I felt like I was "Drivin' My Life Away."

The first weekend in October I was working back in New Hampshire. I took a long ride up to the White Mountains Saturday afternoon to check out the best fall foliage I'd seen in a few years. A lot of people were on the road "leaf peeping," and I was one of the crowd taking pictures at various stops. Just as the sun was setting, I needed gas. I pulled into a convenience store near North Conway where they had a lot of pumps. I had to go inside and wait in line to pay cash after I filled up the Rusty Volare with regular gas. When I came back out to the car, I noticed the flap was open. Some prick stole my gas cap! I asked a couple of people who were out there pumping gas for their vehicles, and they said they didn't see anybody take it. Fortunately, I had a rag in the back seat and I stuffed in to the hole, shut the lid, and drove 100 miles south to my apartment. There were no auto parts stores open on Sunday, so I had to wait until my lunch hour from work on Monday to get one. It was a long winter, and I kept fighting the slow battle with the rust on the fenders. I couldn't bring myself to crawl and look at the undercarriage. Salt on the roads didn't help the situation, either.

1981 was the last year I went back and forth to Florida, and the car turned the 80,000-mile mark in June. I was having no further problems with the Rusty Volare until my 34th birthday in May. That day I was going to drive up to Montreal, check into a hotel, and go out and have a good time at some of my old haunts. At about 3 o'clock on I-89, I had to use my brakes a couple of times, and they started squealing loudly. I got off the interstate and made it to South Burlington where I brought it into a Sears Automotive, since I had a Sears credit card. They didn't look really busy, but after two hours of waiting, I was wondering what the hell the problem was that it was taking so long. The manager gave me the runaround about the right kind of front brake pads they had to install (which I suspected was an untruth), but they finally got the job done just before 6 o'clock when they closed. It was too late to go to Montreal, so I decided to check into a motel there, have dinner, and see what night life Burlington had to offer. I grumbled to myself about not getting to Montreal after the first place that I went to was dead. The second place had more people, and at the bar I met a lady who helped me celebrate my birthday to the max for the rest of the evening. In fact, I spent that whole weekend with her. So, I silently thanked the Rusty Volare and the bullshitters at that Sears automotive for the stroke of good luck that was worth the price of the repairs.

Three months later, on my way back from Florida, I decided to take a slower, alternate route up north after visiting a friend in Charlotte, N.C. On I-81, just outside of Wilkes-Barre, PA, there was another major incident with the Rusty Volare, and this time my luck was the opposite of what transpired in May. I was cruising along and suddenly heard a loud, scraping noise, so I pulled off to the side of the road close to an exit. I couldn't bend down very far to see underneath the car without getting hit, but the glimpse I had of the undercarriage elicited a scream to anyone who may have been listening.

"Oh shit! I probably need a muffler or maybe even a muffler and manifold repair!"

Somehow, after laying sparks as I got off the exit, I made it to a place called Harris Muffler. After my rust hunk of metal crawled into the shop, the guy who checked it out said the catalytic converter was just about rotted away and that caused the scraping sound.

The service desk man remarked, "Your whole exhaust system could use an overhaul, buddy."

"I don't have much money on me and my credit card is almost maxed out."

"A new catalytic converter and exhaust system, for what you need, will run you at least $400 with labor."

"No way can I afford that. Can't you put in some kind of pipe instead, and I'll get it fixed when I get back to New Hampshire?"

"I could take it off and connect everything with a thrush pipe instead of the catalytic converter for around $70. But you better get one before your inspection comes up. It's illegal not to have one in most states nowadays."

"Go ahead and take it off. Connect the pipes. $70 or so is about what I can afford because I have no choice. This thing isn't due for inspection until November."

I had about $150 in my wallet. I thought, "Too bad I didn't stay in Florida and get a job there. They just did away with their inspection laws. My landlord in Florida even fused a Speed Limit sign to his wife's lopsided Chevette in place of a door, and he got it running again."

A few hours later I was back on the road and stayed at my mother's house that night. I called Van the next day to tell him of my ordeal. He was living in Clifton Park now, after getting divorced last year.

"Meet me at the Rusty Nail for lunch," he said.

I got to the Rusty Nail first and I noticed Van looking underneath the car in the parking lot as I was sitting at the bar. He came in and smiled as he sat down next to me.

I said, "I saw you out there crawling out from underneath this rustmobile. How bad does it look?"

"They did a good job, but at some point, you're gonna need a new muffler and a catalytic converter. But overall, it isn't that bad – just rust in spots, no holes yet. The manifold is OK."

"Thank God. Think it'll make it through next winter all right?"

"Yeah, but you never know. You could never get that to pass inspection without a catalytic converter. Do you know any old gas stations or garages in New Hampshire where it would pass inspection from them as it is?"

"No, but I'll ask around. I'll go anywhere in about a 35-mile radius or so, if I have to. There's got to be some sleazy little place somewhere that would pass it. Or I'll have to sell it and get another junk car. I really don't want to do that, though. I'd rather buy a new one at some point. Hell, I just got through paying off the loans on this piece of crap."

"I know what you mean. I had a loan on my '79 Plymouth Sapporo – good car, but a deer slammed into it last winter."

"I'm still gonna be paying for school, too. The GI Bill can only pay for so much and the 10-year limit expires next year for me. I moved so much in the last few years that the bank lost track of me. Sooner or later, they'll find me for the loan, though."

"At least you're not divorced with a kid, like I am."

"But I'm almost flat broke. I have to get back to my job and get a paycheck."

Two months later, I was at a happy hour at the Ramada Inn downtown with a few people from work. We got talking about cars, and when I brought up the tales of woe about the Rusty Volare, one guy said that he knew of a gas station about 5 miles outside of town that would pass any car's inspection. A few days later, I went out there to get gas.

Inside I asked the old guy behind the desk, "Hey, could you inspect my car? It's missing a catalytic converter."

He replied, "Bring it in. I'm the judge of what's hazardous in a car and what isn't. I've owned this business here for 30 years and I don't like any of these damn government regulations."

"It's not due for about another month."

"Call here after Halloween and make an appointment. Ask for Ted. That's me."

"Thanks, Ted, I appreciate your help."

I called him on November 2nd and brought it in that Friday afternoon. The Rusty Volare passed with flying colors, according to Ted, as he posted the sticker inside the windshield.

One Saturday, in early January, I was driving to Dolph's house about 10 miles away – he invited me to see an NFL playoff football game and have dinner with his family. Just as I got outside of town right after the sun went down, a humungous snow squall came from out of nowhere in a matter of minutes. All of a sudden it turned into a virtual blizzard. I could hardly see, on top of it being dark. Cars were skidding on the Interstate and the Rusty Volare started to stall. It skidded and slid into a shallow ditch. I climbed out of the passenger side of the car and ambled along for about a mile in white-out conditions on the side of the road, hoping nobody would hit me or the car. A couple of people blasted their horns at me. One drunken (or stoned) bitch in a car's passenger seat rolled down her window and yelled, "There's no sidewalk here, asshole!" I soon trudged through a small field to a shopping center – my shoes, socks, and part of my pants were soaked. I cursed myself for forgetting to renew my AAA membership a month earlier. There was a pay phone outside of a grocery store, and I called Dolph.

He said, "Where are you? We're just about ready to eat dinner."

"Have you looked outside? It's snowing like hell! This wasn't supposed to happen. My goddamn piece of crap car is in a ditch about a mile north of Shaw's (grocery store). I'm at Shaw's now. I'm going inside to stay warm."

"Ernie (his father-in-law) and I will come and get you."

"Go ahead and eat without me. I'll have a sandwich later. I'll stay inside here near the cashiers. Bring a couple of shovels."

I bought a half pound of ham, a small loaf of sliced Italian bread, a cake, and a 6-pack of beer in the store – for anyone at Dolph's house who wished to partake. They got to Shaw's 45 minutes later. I hopped in the back seat, and the snow suddenly stopped.

"Dolph, Ernie – thanks so much. I'm sorry this happened. You guys are lifesavers."

Dolph said, "There are a couple of other cars off the road. It's amazing this storm came up so fast and then it just stopped. Look, it's clear now."

Ernie chimed in, "You missed a good first half – the Dolphins and Chargers. You missed a good meal, too."

"Hey, I got ham, bread, and dessert for everybody, and some beer for us to share."

When we got to the car, I put it in Neutral and the three of us pushed it out. Fortunately, there was hardly any traffic. I quickly jumped in the car, and the Rusty Volare started up. I beeped my horn and waved at them, and I was on my way to Dolph's house, pulling into his driveway 15 minutes later. They already had some beer and wine there. I watched the rest of the game and talked with their family as I ate two sandwiches and some cake. I also drank almost all of the 6-pack of beer over the next two and a half hours and passed out on the couch. I didn't wake up until the next morning, hung over.

The rest of 1982 into 1983 for the Rusty Volare featured the usual series of tune-ups, shocks and struts, tires, and deteriorating fabric inside the car. Even more rust was starting to show, too. Book value on the car was crashing. I started putting away money toward a new car, hoping I could buy something much better in the next year or two. However, the bank with whom I negotiated my student loan in 1979 finally found me (after all the changes of residences and phone numbers I had made), and I had to make regular payments to them for the next 7 years.

The next major issue with the Volare occurred in the summer of 1983. I happened to be home for a 3-day weekend and my brother and I were at a mall in Colonie, NY on Friday morning. After we came out of the mall, we got into the car and when I went to turn on the ignition, I heard a "click, click, click." The horn didn't work, either. Fortunately, we were parked at the end of the mall about 40 yards away from the Sears automotive center. We put it in neutral and pushed it over there as far as the back of the Sears parking lot while other drivers on the narrow road that we had to get across were cursing us, louder than we were cursing the Rusty Volare.

After stumbling inside, almost out of breath, I told the guy at the desk, "I think it's the battery or the starter. It's the original battery – at the 116,000-mile mark."

My brother added, "He had a lot of trips a lot of trips back and forth to Florida."

The guy behind the counter looked incredulous at us. "I have to see it to believe it."

When he opened up the hood and saw the Mopar name, he said, "Wow – I'm impressed."

I replied, "The battery's been the only impressive thing about this car. I want to get a Die Hard. The cheapest one appropriate for the car, because I'll probably get rid of it next year."

"If there's a Hall of Fame for batteries, this one should go in there. From what I've seen, most batteries from cars like yours die in 3 or 4 years and nobody ever gets more than 60 to 70 thousand miles out of them."

"I wish the suspension system and tires lasted that long."

He laughed. "Those things on cars like yours keeps us in business. We'll get 'er done, but it'll be about a couple of hours."

After walking in and out of every store in the mall and having lunch nearby, we walked back and had to wait another 45 minutes before we were on the road again. It was totally my fault that I didn't replace the battery sooner. "From now on, I'm not going any more than about 4 or 5 years or around 50,000 miles without a new battery – ever again," I thought.

About 6 weeks later, I was supposed to go to New York City for a party to see a lady I knew from college who had just come up to visit me a few weekends earlier. I planned to drive over to Rensselaer, New York, about 150 miles away, to park the car and take the train down to New York City. However, two nights before I was to leave, the radiator blew and one of the hoses cracked. I called all service stations and car repair shops in the area and I couldn't get an appointment to get the damn thing fixed until Monday. I couldn't get a hold of her, either. I felt so depressed I took a 4-day "mental health" weekend off. My friend from New York, Mort, called me Sunday morning.

"Hey, what happened to you? You didn't show up for the party. You were supposed to be the guest of honor at Sara's place."

I told him what happened and said, "The guest of honor? Honor for what? Nobody honors me for anything. Now I'm really embarrassed. I blew it again with her – worse than back in college. She's not gonna want to see me again."

"Anyway, I think she was disappointed. When are you gonna make it down here again?"

"I don't know. It may be a long time. The Rusty Volare put a stake through my heart, figuratively. I'll probably go home to my mother's for Christmas, and if I have a problem with the car my friend Van can help me, but otherwise I don't want to take this car much outside of the area. I'll try to call Sara today. I don't think she has an answering machine. If I can't get a hold of her, I'll write to her."

"If I see her first, I'll tell her what happened."

"She probably won't believe it."

The upshot was that it was $450 down the drain and Sara soon met another guy and married him a few years later (I met him – he's a real good guy. Sara and I are still friends today.).

That wasn't the end of the Volare, though. In March, I was supposed to fly down to Florida to get my degree, but there was a 2-day blizzard in Boston. Ordinarily I could've made it in time to get the prized sheepskin, even with delays, but the damn unreliable crapster wouldn't turn over because the starter burned out. No re-fund for the flight, and the starter cost $65 plus labor. Surprisingly, the Rusty Volare presented no real problems over the next 6 months. I moved to Albany to take a great temporary job (an internship), but with a huge cut in salary.

A month after I started living in Albany, I was supposed to meet my brother for lunch downtown when the damn car inexplicably died as I pulled into a parking space near the restaurant. I called the nearest AAA dealer. After he hooked up the car to tow it to his garage, which was 4 or 5 blocks away, the bar slipped off the tow truck and put a huge dent in the right fender. Some rust scattered on the ground.

"Oh, Jeez," I said, downheartedly. "I need to get in the car to get something out of the glove compartment."

"Sir, I'm so sorry. This was my fault."

I pulled a camera out of the glove compartment and quickly snapped a couple of photos.

He excitedly said, "Look, I'll fix the dent for you. I do my own body work and painting, and I'll do it for free. You don't have to go through insurance."

"How long'll it take to get the job done?"

"I promise that I'll have it done in 3 days, and I'll get it running, too."

"OK, it's a deal," I said. I figured that I would have enough money saved to buy a new car if the rusty Volare made it through the winter, allowing for around $600 in future expenses if Van could help, and I might get $500 on a trade-in if I bought the cheapest, most reliable Chrysler corporation car I could get.

My brother, who had a law office in downtown Albany, gave me a ride to work for the next few days. As promised, the tow truck man called me three days later and I went over to pick up the car. "I got the engine running, too. I hope you like it," he said.

"Good job. Thank you," I replied, as I shook his hand. Actually, the job was just "OK," but given the age and condition of the vehicle, and that it was running, I couldn't complain.

Right after New Years' Day, 1985, I started to have problems with the brakes, and I needed a new master cylinder. Van wasn't able to help because he was coping with an injury. Another $350 flew out of my wallet. There were no more problems with the Volare for the next 3 months, however, and I was glad the rustmobile stayed alive through another winter. One morning in April, the engine started running rough on the way home from work. I thought, "Uh oh. Maybe transmission problems are looming. This sounds like the Flameout Astre before I dumped it."

I called Van, who came over and said, "Yeah. I think it might be the transmission going. It could be other things, though."

Before he could get another word out of his mouth, I said, "That's it. I'm getting the Consumer Reports car issue that came out this month. I have enough money to get rid of this fucking thing once and for all. It's stupid to just keep sinking money into it."

After our usual pizza and beer, I went to a store on Central Avenue that sold various newspapers and magazines and bought the last copy of Consumer Reports on the rack. I hustled back to my apartment, jotted down a few possibilities and settled on buying a new '85 Dodge Colt. Over the next couple of days, I went to a few dealers in the area, and I really liked test driving the Colt. Van had recommended the Dodge dealer in Schenectady who had exactly what I wanted – a comfortable hatchback with a Mitsubishi AM/FM stereo cassette player.

After I test drove it, I asked, "How much will you give me on the trade-in for the Volare (hoping $400 would be a great deal)? I can throw in a lot of cash up front. My mother's a bank officer and I can get a 1-year loan through her bank for the balance."

The salesman responded, "Let's see what the boss says."

"He said $600 for the trade-in."

"You got it."

"Let's go inside, talk over the details, and sign on the dotted lines."

I filled out all the paperwork – this time I had the title for the Volare with me.

I asked, "I can drive it home, then?"

He said, "There is some dealer prep involved – $95. But we can deliver it to you at work tomorrow just before noon."

The next day at 11 a.m., I noticed two guys in the parking lot – one of them pulled in with the Colt. I dropped what I was doing and went outside to greet them.

"It's yours. You'll like how surprisingly peppy this little car is," one guy said as the other handed me the keys. They both shook my hand, and it was official – the untrusty, Rusty Volare was gone for good. I called Van and we celebrated with pizza and beer that evening.

CHAPTER 7

The Good 20th Century Cars I Bought: 1985-2000

The little 4-cylinder tan 1985 Dodge Colt made by Mitsubishi ran great, handled great, had good brakes, got good gas mileage, the AM/FM/Cassette sound system was excellent, and the ride was comfortable. Plus, the hatchback provided sufficient storage when I needed it. The summer of '85 proved to be pleasurable driving with no worries of any kind of breakdowns.

I moved to Maryland that September and drove the hell out of it because I had a female friend in Salisbury, and I really liked hanging out in Ocean City most weekends. The day before Thanksgiving I drove it back to my mother's house in upstate NY and it started snowing just as I got there – 8 inches overnight. But I had no problems getting it on the road with minimal shoveling the next afternoon. Right after I got back to Maryland, I went out to eat at a fast-food place for lunch and a truck threw up a stone that put a small crack in the windshield. About an hour after I got back, I went outside to check on it and the whole passenger side of the windshield developed cracks in it. I thought, "Here we go, again – my first goddammit with this car." I called Safelite and they did the whole job in less than 2 hours. It wiped out the deductible for my insurance, but I wasn't going anywhere until my next paycheck, anyway.

In March I moved to a city 30 miles away, and the commute to work ran up more miles on the car, but I was happily driving it all over Maryland, D.C., Delaware, parts of Virginia, and Philadelphia every few weekends. From April to October of '86 I had a girlfriend 60 miles away in Dover, DE and I saw her every weekend. The Colt ran like a top. No problems. "Best car I ever had," I thought, in spite of some other problems in my personal and work life.

Two months after the relationship broke up, I was driving in upstate NY to visit my mother and relatives over the Christmas holidays for a week and a half. Because there were accidents all over the place in northern New Jersey and southern New York, I decided to take an alternate route toward the Taconic State Parkway, a car three cars up from me suddenly stopped to make a U-turn. Just as my car slowed to a stop – *"POW!"* Some bastard in a Jeep Wrangler hit me in the right rear of my car and suddenly there was a chain reaction of crashes in the cars in front of me, causing a pile-up. The son-of-a-bitch in the Wrangler didn't even stop! I felt shook up and got the worst of it, but the other cars also got damaged. All of us exited our cars as I screamed out a few curse words. I was almost in tears and then the cops came. It was obvious that my poor Dodge Colt was totaled, and they towed it to a junkyard. I was pissed, but what could I do? The guy in the tow truck gave me a ride from there to an Amtrak station that wasn't very many miles away, which was nice of him. I took my bags with me and told him I would come down and pick up the rest of the stuff in the car the next morning. I called home when I got to the Croton-Harmon train station and my brother wondered if I was in a state of shock from the way I was talking. I assured him I was OK. He said he would pick me up at the station in Rensselaer around 8 p.m. Then I called my insurance agent who asked for all the details, and which police had the official report, etc. He said he would get back to me after the weekend. If the car was totaled (it sure looked like it), he would arrange for an adjuster to examine it and get me a rental car from a place near where I lived in Maryland.

The next morning, I called Van. "Van. I'm home. I got the shit smashed out me last night on the way and the car is totaled."

"Are you all right? What happened?"

"I have a wicked whiplash – my neck and shoulders. Otherwise, I'm OK. There was a lot of traffic and supposedly some accidents in New Jersey and near the Thruway, so I decided to be clever and go from Saw Mill Run Parkway to I-287 to get to the Taconic State Parkway when I was at the rear of a 4-car pileup because some asshole in a Jeep Wrangler rammed into my right rear fender hard and took off. The shithead was probably drunk."

"Where's the car now?"

It got towed to a junkyard not far away from there. No way was it drivable."

"Aw, you're fucked again. That's a damn shame. The best car you ever had, too."

"What are you doing today?"

"Nothing. Maybe some laundry later."

"I need a favor. How'd you like to drive a couple hours or so down to the junkyard so I can get the rest of my stuff out of the car?"

"Why the hell didn't you didn't get it all?"

"Well, I have one large suitcase and a smaller bag I jammed as much stuff in as I could. Good thing it was a hatchback. I never would've got the trunk open. I want to talk to them there, anyway. I promise I'll buy the pizza and beer when we get back. If you can't do it, I'll ask my brother to see if he'll drive me there."

"No, I'll do it. I didn't get a chance to see you over Thanksgiving, anyway. I need a break from Liz (his wife of 3 years), anyway. You can tell me all about what happened with Sue Ann (my ex-girlfriend) last month."

"Can you meet me at my mother's house in about an hour?"

"I'll be there."

"Thanks a lot, Van. See you then."

We went to the junkyard, catching up on the way down about a variety of things that happened in our lives over the prior few months. As he drove in, we creeped past about 50 or 60 wrecked cars on the muddy dirt road up to the office. A Doberman Pinscher growled as we came in. The owner was there, I told him who I was, that my car was towed there last night, and I wanted to get the rest of my stuff out of it.

"I need to see your license, registration, and your insurance card."

"Here's my license and insurance. I left the registration in the glove compartment."

"We got it. I just wanted to make sure it was you. The insurance adjuster is coming on Tuesday. You didn't leave the key, so I need that. Your vehicle is open."

After I gave him the key, he said, "I know you're from Maryland, but can you give me the phone number of where you're staying in New York so I can get a hold of you, or so the insurance adjuster can?"

"Yeah, sure."

He pointed to the row where the car was. The Doberman stayed quiet with him. Van and I got the rest of my stuff out of the Colt – what a sad sight, as I turned away from the fabulous little car. The right rear was crumpled up like an accordion. I almost cried.

Van said, "Wow! You really do have shit luck with cars. You have a picture of it, don't you?"

"Only a partial one when it was parked at work. I sure as hell wouldn't want to take a picture of it now."

We didn't talk much on the way back – just various small talk about cars, mainly. The pizza and beer at a Pizza Hut later seemed like a meal after a funeral. The insurance company people called me a few days later, and the car was definitely a total loss. They would be sending me a check for a little over $4000 in the near future and arranged for me to get a rental car in Maryland that I could pick up a couple days after New Year's.

"Thanks for your help," I dismissively said to the voice on the other end of the phone.

"What a Merry fuckin' Christmas," I thought.

The rental car turned out to be another white Chevy – this time an '82 Chevy Cavalier coupe. Visibility in it was poor, it didn't have a rear window defroster, and at times, a bike probably had more power. But it got me to and from work, at least. When I finally got my insurance check a few weeks later (after much bitching over the phone as to what was taking so long for it to get to me), I went out looking for another vehicle. I finally bought a brand-new '87 Honda Civic Wagon in late January.

The Honda Civic wagon was another good car. It was a copper colored 4-cylinder automatic that got excellent gas mileage, lots of room to store things when the rear seat folded down, and comfortable. The only misgiving I had was that I got it without air conditioning because I had a job interview in Vermont right after Christmas that went so well that I thought I wouldn't need that, or even power steering. But the job didn't come through for me and I wound up spending the next 28 years living in either Maryland or Delaware. The first year I had the Civic Wagon I piled up a lot of miles on the car because I became involved in a long-distance relationship with a lady from back in New Hampshire who started living with me the next year. I married her the year after that.

I was living in Delaware in August 1989. At the 48,000-mile mark, just as we were about to go on vacation, the Civic Wagon's battery started dying. AAA jumped it for me and again, as luck would have it, there was a Sears Automotive a mile away. I bought a Die Hard and we were on our way to Maine, with only a two-hour delay. After we got back from our trip, my wife relinquished her '83 Subaru so we could buy an '89 Eagle Summit. I had a full-time job, and she did not, although she was about to start one. Grudgingly, she took the Civic Wagon (intermittently bitching about the lack of power steering) and the Eagle Summit was mine. However, at times we drove both cars interchangeably, except when I drove a total of 55 miles back and forth to work every day.

One afternoon in 1991 I got a frantic call from her as I was about to leave work. She angrily yelled, "I need you right now! I'm stuck in the parking lot of the bank with an 11-year-old and something's definitely wrong under the hood. I think it's starting to smoke up."

"I'm leaving now. I'll be right over there."

"Can you get here in 20 minutes?"

"No way – it always takes me at least a half hour to get home."

"Well, I have to call AAA now!"

She hung up. She wasn't at the bank when I got there, so I went home. When I walked in the door she said, grouchily, "They told me the water pump blew." The Civic Wagon had been towed to a nearby garage, and they said they would put in a new one tomorrow. It wound up costing $300. At that point, the Civic Wagon had 91,000 miles on it. But that was it for any major repairs made to the Civic Wagon. After the car turned 122,000 miles in June 1993, I sold it to Don in Pittsburgh.

In the meantime, the '89 Eagle Summit turned out to be an excellent car. It was a maroon 4-door sedan that was a Chrysler/Mitsubishi product that was supposed to be a replacement for the Dodge Colt. Aside from the battery dying after 40,000 miles, I had absolutely no problems with this little sedan. In fact, my wife bought a new light blue Eagle Summit right after we sold the Civic Wagon to Don (however, after a while, her Eagle Summit had intermittent problems with the brakes and several years later she traded it in for a Honda Civic).

But I got greedy. Someone zoomed by me in a new '93 Honda Civic Del Sol on the road a couple of weeks after she bought her car and I thought, "Hey, my Eagle Summit has over 70,000 miles on it. Why not get a faux sports car like that Del Sol for a change? I have the money." I went up to visit my mother one July weekend, and as my brother and I were coming back from playing golf outside of Troy, NY, I noticed a Honda dealer.

I demanded, "Pull over. I want to test drive one of those new Del Sols."

He said, "All right. What the hell; I don't have anything to do for another hour or so. You're not gonna buy one of those things right now, anyway."

"Oh, no. I'd never buy one here. Remember you test drove all those cars years ago that you had no intention of buying?"

"Yeah. That was fun."

The salesman came out right away.

I said, "Hi, I'd like to test drive one of these Del Sols you have here."

"Sure thing. Can I see your driver's license?"

"Here it is."

"Delaware. What are you doing up here?"

"Visiting my brother here for the weekend."

"You got something you want to trade?"

Danny said, "This is my car we came in (a '91 Toyota Camry)."

"I see the New York plates, but what'd you drive to get up here?"

"An '89 Eagle Summit. If I think I want to buy the Del Sol, I'll bring it here later."

He suddenly remembered that he played hockey against Danny in high school and briefly in a semi-pro league 10 years after that. They talked about hockey and people they knew for a couple minutes. He seemed to feel easier about letting me test drive a Del Sol.

"All right, let me get the demo we've been using, and I'll slap on some plates for you."

He brought around this psychedelic green colored Del Sol. He demonstrated how the roof, which weighed 24 pounds, was detachable and put in the trunk, which was spacious for such a sporty little car. He gave me the keys. I started it up and we took off for a 3- to 4-mile drive.

"Ooh, this thing is peppy. Pretty comfortable, too," I said.

"Geez, I like it. Maybe you should buy this one," Danny replied.

"Nah. The color is weird. But I do have a clipboard that matches it," I laughed.

"There are some hills and curves up ahead. Let's see how it does."

We zoomed and twisted a little through the two-lane country road for about a mile. It was a joyful ride. I had never driven anything close to a sports car before.

I said, "I like the way this thing handles. The brakes are good, too."

"I'll turn on the radio."

A couple oldies songs came on the FM station as we drove. "Good sound. Probably even better with the top in," I said, smilingly.

"It looks like you have good visibility."

"Yeah, but when I bring it back, I have to complain about something, or the guy could easily talk me into buying this one right now."

We drove back to the dealer. The salesman, with a smile, asked, "Well, what d'ya think?"

"I replied, "It's a good little car, and there are a lot of things I like, but it runs loud, the visibility is probably not as good with the roof in, and I hate the color. I'd have to put a new radio in, too."

He told us about how overwhelming the positives to the vehicle were, but I told him that I'd keep looking. "Besides, I am living in Delaware."

"But you won't have to pay the sales tax, even though you'd buy it here."

"I'll take your card. Thanks, anyway."

We got in the car and left. I said to Danny, "He almost had me. Besides, I like the guy, and he didn't seem like a sociopath. A lot of car salespeople are."

"I think you should get one, but a different color."

The day after I got back home, I traded in the maroon Eagle Summit and bought a black Del Sol. In 7 years, I put almost 150,000 miles on it and there was only one thing that went wrong with it. The first few times I drove it in fairly heavy rain, or when I went to wash it, the corner of the roof on the driver's side dripped slowly, with the water landing high up on my left leg. I had to squirm to avoid looking like I peed in my pants. I took it back to the dealership and I got an apology, telling me that the moldings connecting the roof may have been made a tiny bit too large. The service department promptly corrected the problem, and I never had a problem with it again.

The Del Sol was the best car I ever had in the 20th century. It looked like my crap car days were finally over, after 3 good cars in a row.

CHAPTER 8

Wait, There's More! 1999: the Year of the Feisty Festiva

The Del Sol still ran well in 1999, but my office was moving to a high crime area in May. To preserve the Del Sol against possible damage, I thought I wanted to get as good resale value as possible in the future, even though I was racking up about 20,000 miles a year on the Del Sol. I decided to look for a cheap, but reliable non-descript, air-conditioned older vehicle with good gas mileage to drive a total of 55 miles back and forth to work, if such a car existed. I could afford about $1500 max. I called Van, and then Don, and also started looking over the internet in February. Van couldn't come up with anything. Don, who was heavily into buying, fixing up, and selling cars for a lot of years now, wanted me to purchase an '88 Ford Taurus that he had. "It has 120,000 miles on it, but the interior is very good, and it runs like a top," he told me.

"If I can't get anything else in the next week or so, I'll take you up on it, if you still got it."

"OK. I'll keep looking for you, though."

A couple of nights later, I went on the internet and noticed that someone about 20 miles south of Pittsburgh was selling a '90 Ford Festiva that had everything I wanted. I called Don, who said he'd check it out right away.

Don excitedly called me back two days later, saying, "You have to come out here and get this car. It's a steal of a deal. They are a nice old couple selling it, and it's probably worth a lot more. I put $100 down on it to them, so if you don't want it, I'll buy it. I told them you'd probably be here Saturday."

I said, "Great! I'll try to get a one-way flight as cheap as I can for Saturday morning and we can go down there."

My wife and I had an argument about such a possibly fool-hardy adventure. However, come Saturday morning I was in a plane taking off for Pittsburgh. Don met me at the airport.

"How was your flight?"

"Very smooth and I got a great deal on a one-way fare."

"Let's go. Their place is about a half an hour away, out in the country."

"I'm glad it's 35-degree gray day weather. At least it isn't snowing or 20 degrees colder."

We met the nice elderly couple outside. Don said to me, "I drove this the other day. See what you think."

I asked them, "Do you mind if we take it for a little bit of a test drive?"

"Sure, go right ahead."

"We'll be back in 10 minutes."

The car rode well. The heater worked. The air conditioning even worked. It had a rear window defroster. The rear seat folded down, as an adjunct to the trunk space. The radio worked fine. The ride was relatively smooth, but slightly loud – about what you would expect for a 9-year-old car of its size with 80,000 miles on it. No rips in the tan upholstery. No dents and only very minimal rust in the exterior. When we got back, Don opened up the hood, and I crawled underneath the car to see any obvious warning signals.

"Looks good under the hood," Don remarked.

"I might need a muffler in about 3 months or so, but that's all," I replied.

I asked the man, "$1200, right?"

His wife smiled and replied, "Yes, sir.'

"It's a deal. I have the cash right here in my wallet."

"We'll sign it over right now."

A few minutes later, we were on our way downtown to Motor Vehicle. Don told me how to fill out the Pennsylvania forms and temporary registration. By 11:30, I bought him lunch at Primati Brothers.

In the parking lot I said, "I wish I could stay longer, but I have to get back before it gets too dark."

"I have to get back to the house because I have somebody coming to take a look at the Taurus at 1 o'clock."

"Thanks a whole lot, Don. I'll see you in the summer – come on down to Delaware."

"I will. By the way, you look good in that turquoise car."

The 6-hour ride home was smooth despite some rain mixed with snow in part of Maryland. Thank God it wasn't freezing rain. Traffic wasn't bad. I filled up the gas tank only once on the way and I was getting about 35 mpg., even with no cruise control. The lights worked well. I pulled into the driveway of our house a little after 6:30 p.m.

I beeped the horn. My wife and stepson came out and she said, "Oh no – you didn't! Turquoise? What an ugly little car!"

My step-son, home from college for the weekend, laughed and declared, "It looks like it came from out of the very back of some used car lot."

"Hey, it's not the Ford Explorer like you have. Besides, Don just told me I look good in turquoise today."

"Yeah, right. You better be driving it to and from work only. I'd be embarrassed to be seen in that thing," my wife said.

"That's all right with me. I was planning on driving it to and from work only and using the Del Sol only on weekends, or maybe even your car (the '98 red Honda Civic)."

The Festiva felt great traveling back and forth to work. Some of my friends at work chuckled, seeing me drive into the parking lot, but I thought "What a good deal I got with this one!" No problems at all during the first four months for the 55-mile round-trip drive from home to work, five days a week. Sure enough, though, one day in June while I went out of the office to eat lunch, I heard the *"blabberty, blab, blab,"* like a tremendously loud, gurgling, farting noise coming out of the rear of the Festiva. I knew what it was right away – the muffler. I called my secretary and told her I had to take at least an hour of the comp time I had coming, "maybe more." I drove the Festiva to a Meineke Muffler shop about a mile away, and they weren't too busy that day, telling me that if I waited, they could get it done in about an hour.

"I hope that's all it needs – not a tailpipe, manifold, or a catalytic converter."

The mechanic took a look under the car and said, No – it looks like you got a rusty hole in your muffler, but everything else is probably OK. We'll let you know."

And that's all it was – I needed a new muffler and nothing else!

"Do you want a new tail pipe put in? We're running a special on a muffler/tail pipe combo. For your car it would cost $119 + tax."

I said, "Sure."

I called the office. "Sandy, if anybody's looking for me, I'll be back at about 2 o'clock. I'm at the Meineke Muffler near the bridge."

My wife and I separated at the end of the month, and I used the Festiva to lug almost all of my stuff to a storage bin about a mile away from my house. It also took me a few trips to move my things from the storage bin to a new apartment 30 miles away in Maryland. A friend of mine, Johnny, had a small pickup truck. He helped me when I drove the Del Sol to his house, and he brought me back to the storage bin where I parked the Festiva. He put some of the larger objects in the truck while the Festiva was loaded down with a bunch of boxes and bags, and the queen-sized mattress on the roof of the car. Thankfully, I was in flat country with no hills and a minimum of curves. I had to drive like a very old man, even putting my flashers on at times. I didn't encounter any cops. The power wavered at times when I tried to drive it over 40 m.p.h.

"C'mon," I yelled to the Festiva, "You're the Little Engine that Could!"

I made it with that load OK.

The second load was just as heavy and 15 miles away from the new apartment, the Festiva was starting to wobble.

"You're like Rocky," I yelled to the feisty little car. "You're gonna go the distance!"

Really, I was wondering if I was wrecking the Festiva's shocks and springs. I had to pull over and stop twice. But the last load was no problem.

After I unloaded the last of my belongings, I patted the Festiva on the hood and said, "I'm glad I bought you. You are one tough little son of a bitch."

As it turned out, miraculously, I didn't need new shocks or springs. There was smooth sailing back and forth to work with the Feisty Festiva all through the summer into the fall. The gas mileage, the air conditioning, and the radio/cassette player all made a 25-mile round trip commute one a comfortable ride.

One day after work in October, I had to go back over to my wife's house to settle a matter about taking our dog, Max, for the weekend. After an argument, I left and drove back to my apartment in Maryland. It was getting dark, and I had just about calmed down from the confrontation about 2 or 3 miles away from my place. Out of the corner of my eye, I suddenly saw a large animal speeding across a field on the right edge of the road.

I screamed, *"Noooo!"*

Then – *"Whap!"* Just as I had started to hit the brakes, a fairly big horned buck slammed into my right front fender, bounced off it and kept on going, as the Festiva went into the other lane. Good thing no other cars were coming. After uttering some curse words, I thought, "This is what Evel Knievel must've felt like after one of his failed stunts." But the Feisty Festiva and I were still alive and the car limped home, smoking up for the last quarter mile. Luckily, no cops stopped me; just before I left my wife's, I had just downed a 16-ounce beer. There was a big dent in the passenger side door and the whole right front fender was smashed in – you could see some of the buck's white hair wedged into the front of the door.

The next day I called in sick because the whiplash was worse than what I had back in 1973 with the Green Toad, or 1980 with the Rusty Volare, or in 1986 with the Colt. But the Festiva's injuries were even worse – I knew this was the death knell for it. Evidently, my luck with used cars hadn't changed after all.

I called my insurance company that day. Unlike the other company when I had the accidents in 1980 and 1986, an insurance adjuster came over two days later.

The adjuster asked, "Why didn't you call the police?"

"I thought I could make it home OK – it was only about a few miles away, and the car was still running and moving." I didn't tell him that the last thing I wanted was any suspicion of a DUI, even though I wasn't intoxicated, and I didn't trust the "hanging" state troopers with their recent claims to try to nail people.

"You didn't get hurt?"

"The only bodily injury I got was waking up yesterday morning with a terrible whiplash, but I'm about OK now."

"What proof do you have that you got hit by a deer?"

"Look, here's the evidence – that's deer hair and a smidgen of hide in the jamb of the door."

After inspecting it, he said, "I'll tell you right now, your car is a total loss. Do you have any other transportation you are using?"

"See that black Honda Del Sol over there? That's my other car."

"Good thing the deer didn't hit that instead of the Ford Festiva. I bet that really would've broken your heart." I gave him my cell phone number, as that would be easier to get in touch with me.

"You'll hear from our office sometime next week. In the meantime, someone will come to haul the car away."

On the following Thursday, while I was at work late in the afternoon, I got a call from the insurance office.

"We'd like you to come down to the office before 5 o'clock to pick up your reimbursement check for your car."

"I'll leave right now," I quickly replied.

The place was 30 miles away, and rush hour traffic on U.S. Rt. 50 was just starting. I weaved in and out of cars on the four-lane road and I sped there as quickly as I could, watching for cops along the way. I arrived at the office parking lot about 15 minutes before they closed and dashed inside. As I was signing a few papers, they were giving me some explanations about the documents, and book value on the car, and then they put my reimbursement check in an envelope. I hurriedly said to their questions, "Yeah, Yeah, OK. Thank you very much. I have to get home."

I rushed out of there. I was hoping they'd give me as much as $750 for the Festiva. As I got in the door and approached my car, I opened the envelope and let out a joyful, *"Aaaah! Yes! Hallelujah!"*

The amount of the check read "$1500" for the Feisty Festiva! More than I paid for it back in February! Even with the new tailpipe and muffler in June, I still made almost a couple of hundred dollars on the deal! I went to a restaurant near where I lived and celebrated with a crab cake dinner, the most expensive bottle of imported beer on the menu, and dessert. The next morning, I took a quick 15-minute break from work and deposited the check at my bank. "The Feisty Festiva makes up for all of the junkers I had down through the years," I thought, with a smile.

EPILOGUE

I wanted to drive the Del Sol as little as possible because of the high mileage. Don told me he really wanted to buy it, but he couldn't afford it for a while. I decided to hold it for him for next year, as thanks for helping me with the Festiva. I liked the idea of having two cars, so right before Thanksgiving, I impulsively bought a brand-new 1999 Honda CR-V, putting as much down on it as I could, which turned out to be only a one-year loan. This left me in a big financial hole for the rest of the winter, however (people can do stupid things right after a separation or divorce).

I really liked the green CR-V. It didn't get quite as much gas mileage as I hoped for, although the close to 30 MPG on the highway turned out to be very good for that type of vehicle. This was the dawning of the age of the SUV – more storage space instead of small cars were "in", and one reason I bought it was that I felt I had to "get with it," and get used to any new technology in cars. The full spare tire was attached to the swinging outward trunk – reminiscent of sxzome older Jeeps. It rode very smoothly. Visibility was very good. Even though it was a small to mid-size SUV compared to others on the road, it was the biggest vehicle I ever had, but I felt comfortable with it.

I was at my mother's house over the Christmas holidays, and I had to return a present I bought at a mall outside of Albany. As I drove in the parking lot and hit a STOP sign, behind me I heard a "clunk." The CR-V lunged forward a few inches. A girl rear-ended me with her small vehicle, and she apologized profusely. There was a small dent in my bumper and the tailpipe was slightly bent.

I was a little pissed, to say the least. I said to her, "I have to call the police to investigate this. This is a brand-new car I've only had for a month." Then I realized I forgot to bring my cell phone with me.

I asked, "You got a cell phone?"

Her boyfriend, who looked like a shady character said, "I got one, but it's dead. You don't have to get the cops involved, man."

"Wait right here." I pulled out a pad of paper and a pen from my glove compartment and wrote down her name, driver's license, license plate number, and asked for her address and phone number, which she gave, as her boyfriend sullenly walked away nearby. Then I saw Mall Security patrolling the parking lot, and I ran and got the guy. A state trooper came within a few minutes, investigated the accident.

"You people have your insurance cards with you, I hope?"

"Yeah. Here's mine," I said.

She fumbled through her purse and pulled out a paper card. After the trooper looked at it, I asked, "Can I see that?"

I took a glance at it and quickly wrote down the policy number, which only had 6 digits. Her company was someplace I never heard of in a town near Schenectady.

The trooper issued no charges, and soon after, we were on our way. I reported the accident to my company, and they wanted the other company's information, which I gave. A week later my company called me in Maryland.

Not only had the little bitch's insurance expired, but her company went out of business on December 31st, her phone was disconnected, and she moved out of where she was living, leaving no forwarding address. I figured that she probably sold the car for quick cash because they couldn't find her. My policy with State Farm did not have coverage for uninsured motorists.

"So, I got screwed again. This tops off the miserable year of 1999," I thought. My deductible didn't cover the repair costs, which shockingly came to about $650. This included having the bumper repaired, unlike the Flameout Astre from 24 years earlier. During the summer of 2000 I sold the Del Sol to Don, who promptly sold it to a kid going off to college – he would be driving it out to California.

I had no serious problems with the CR-V over the next 5 years until the early spring of 2005. At that time the CR-V started running rough and it was leaking a little bit of anti-freeze. I was going to look for a new car, but my wife (we got back together in 2001) said that my brother-in-law wanted the car for his son.

"Mike, this has been a good car for me, but it's been running rough lately. I hope there's nothing wrong with it that won't cost you a lot of money. I hope it isn't a blown gasket."

"No, I want it. I know you've taken good care of it."

"Are you sure you want it?"

"Yeah. I'll come over and drive it back to Virginia. I can spend $1000 if the head gasket's blown."

He came over that Saturday and drove it away. In the meantime, my wife bought a brand-new Mazda Miata and gave me her red '98 Honda Civic until I bought a new car.

It turned out to be a cracked engine block. It wasn't worth repairing, and we all were a little upset. That wasn't supposed to happen with a vehicle that had just over 100,000 miles on it, but all the warranties expired. We gave my brother-in-law $1000 if he wanted to fix it. I wrote a complaining letter to Honda and never heard from them.

The '98 Honda Civic was fine for the year I had it, as well as the other 7 years that my wife had driven it. There was never anything seriously wrong with that car. I bought a couple of other excellent cars in the next 5 years: an '06 Mazda-3 and an '11 Subaru Outback. No problems ever with the Mazda-3; I had put 82,000 miles on it in 5 years when I traded it in for a Subaru Outback in March 2011. The first time I drove the Outback home from its initial service, I noticed a rattling a few miles away from my house. As soon as I got home, I opened up the hood and saw a screwdriver hanging around the wires underneath the head. That, indeed, was the problem, and I never took it back to that dealership for service again. I traded in the Subaru Outback after 98,000 miles over 8 years, during which time I had no further problems.

In the pre-pandemic year of 2019, I bought the car I now drive – a '19 Subaru Crosstrek. A couple of internal mishaps cost a total of around $900, but they both were totally my fault. Regarding the first one, I had the vehicle for only 2 weeks when we went to see an open-air play in a park. Just before the performance started a horrendous thunderstorm came up. The play was cancelled, but we had no cover, and had to run back to the car, soaked. I was parked in an open space and when we got in the car a gust of wind came up and blew the heavy rain right into the front seat. We made it home, and I opened all the windows when we got in the garage. The front seat was still damp the next day, so I parked it in the driveway for about 4 hours with all the windows down. Even though it was a warm, sunny day, there was still a damp squishiness when I tried to sit down on the driver's side; however, the passenger side was OK. Then I did a damn dumb thing, which seemed like a good idea at the time – I tried to use a hair drier on the seat. After 2 minutes, a burn with a small rip exposed some of the material underneath the fabric. I went to the dealer; the warranty didn't cover the damage, and I paid about $350 to get an entire new seat cover. I didn't know until later there was stuff called "Damp Rid" I could buy cheaply that would have taken care of the problem. The other incident, 6 months later, involved me accidentally backing into the partially closed garage door while having an argument with my wife, which resulted in getting a new rear window, costing about another $350. However, right after Thanksgiving, 2021, someone sideswiped my left rear bumper in a parking lot in downtown St. Petersburg and took off, but insurance paid for the whole thing, even though the whole bumper had to be replaced. Otherwise, since the 21st century, I have had hardly any problems with my vehicles. The Crosstrek has been about as good as the Outback.

I'm sure a lot of people can identify with what I went through for all those years with the defective cars I had. With some of them, problems were expected – a matter of time. With some of the others, I got fooled big time. Even though at the time, I was mostly cursing, I can look back and laugh at the Vomit Comet and hanging on to the Rusty Volare. I actually had more luck than heartache with the Chirping Cricket and the Feisty Festiva. I have grumbling memories of the Flameout Astre and the '99 CR-V. I deserved what I got with the original Lambmobile and the Green Toad Falcon. When I think of the '85 Colt, it's heartbreaking. That one and most of the others I had from 1987 on, I would buy again in a heartbeat.

The lessons I learned are that it's probably better to buy new or pre-owned certified, and do your homework via Consumer Reports, some reputable car magazine, or maybe Carfax if you want a reliable vehicle.

Secondly, know a good mechanic or car buff like Van or Don who can give good advice, especially if you are buying a used car. Otherwise, with a car bought new, take it to a dealer at prescribed intervals for service, if their service department has a good reputation.

Barring an accident (God forbid), it looks like I might have one more car in my future at some point (mainly to keep up with the technology, like I did by trading in the Outback after 8 years). Here's hoping I have no more bad luck with any future car I buy.

ABOUT THE AUTHOR

P.J. LAMB is a retired mental health professional living in Florida. From 1968 to the present, he has owned 16 different cars, half of which were either junkers or eventually became damaged. He is a sports fan who enjoys 20th century music, walking on the beach at low tide and regularly posting topics on his free and bare bones alongtimeago.blog.

BOOKS BY P.J. LAMB

Taking the Local Train (2019)

Midge's Irish (2023)

www.ingramcontent.com/pod-product-compliance
Lightning Source LLC
Chambersburg PA
CBHW021118130626
46554CB00002B/759